Edinburgh Bilingual Library (7)

EDINBURGH   BILINGUAL   LIBRARY   (7)

Sonnets

LOUISE LABÉ

INTRODUCTION AND COMMENTARIES BY
PETER SHARRATT

TRANSLATIONS BY
GRAHAM DUNSTAN MARTIN
University of Edinburgh

UNIVERSITY   OF   TEXAS   PRESS,   AUSTIN

International Standard Book Number 0-292-74603-2
Library of Congress Catalog Card Number 72-2042
Copyright © 1972 by Peter Sharratt and G. D. Martin
All Rights Reserved

Printed in Great Britain by W & J Mackay Limited, Chatham

Edinburgh Bilingual Library

FOREWORD

An imperfect knowledge of a language need be no bar to reading a work written in it if there is a good translation to help. This Library may aid those who have a wide-ranging and adventurous interest in literature to jump the hurdles of language and thus do something to help break down the barriers of specialization. That it may be helpful for courses in Comparative Literature is our hope, but not our main aim. We wish to appeal to a wider audience: first to the cultivated, serious reader of literature who is not content to remain within the English language, secondly to university students and teachers of English and of Modern Languages by inviting them to throw from outside some new light on, perhaps even discover different values in, their particular fields of specialization.

As this Bilingual Library grows it will try to map, in a necessarily limited and modest way, small areas of Western Literature through the comparison of actual texts. This it will do by building up groups of volumes to illustrate literary traditions, themes and styles. Thus No. 3, *Troubadour Lyric Poetry*, will be followed by volumes of *Minnesang*, Petrarch, Ausias March and others, which together will chart the range and significance of Courtly Love. From time to time volumes will be paired to show literary development across countries and periods. Thus, the technical and conceptual development in the reworking of classical mythology will be shown by the simultaneous publication of Poliziano's *Orfeo* and Góngora's *Polifemo*—the one at the beginning, the other at the end, of the age of Humanism.

The languages represented will be French (with Provençal),

German, Italian, Portuguese, Russian, Spanish (with Catalan), and Medieval and Renaissance Latin. The translations will not be 'cribs' but good literature worth publishing in its own right. Verse will be translated into verse, except where the unfamiliarity of the language for most readers (Provençal, Catalan, Old French, Old High German) may make a more literal prose rendering advisable. In the majority of cases the Introductions will present up-to-date assessments of each author or work, or original interpretations on a scholarly level. Works already accessible in translation will only be included when we think we can offer new translations of special excellence.

A. A. Parker
GENERAL EDITOR

Contents

for Anne-Louise

Louise Labé
Sonnets

PREFACE
There are many people I should thank for help and advice in
the preparation of this book. I wish particularly to thank the
two groups of students who studied Louise Labé with me as
an Honours Special Subject; they will perhaps recognize in
the commentary how much I am indebted to them. I wish to
thank Professor Alan Steele for a kind and helpful reading of
the manuscript, and for making many useful improvements.
A word should also be said about the relation between the
commentary and the translation. These were at first prepared
independently, and then we conferred on points of detail.
There are several places in the commentary where the
translator, Mr Martin, wished to add something to my notes;
I have marked the more important of these additions with an
asterisk. For the rest I am indebted to him for advice and
emendations on many other points, so that the work is the
result of a fruitful collaboration.   PETER SHARRATT

A Note on the Translation
Some special difficulties face the translator of poetry from a
century other than his own. Should he couch his translation
in the contemporary English of the period, as André Pézard
did when he translated Dante into medieval French? Or
should he attempt an equivalent in the poetry of his own
time, as Peter Whigham has done for Catullus? Some poets
lend themselves more to one of these approaches than to the
other, but each has its special dangers. If one attempts the
first solution of the problem, for example, one is likely to end
up with mere pastiche. (Pézard's Dante is here a brilliant
exception.) If one attempts the second . . . well, is the

sonnet even a twentieth-century form? And then, the sixteenth century had a completely different approach to cliché.
We now flee it like the plague; *they* were perhaps as conscious of it as we, but cultivated it deliberately, bent it to their
purposes. I have consequently engaged in various compromi-
ses: I have tried to freshen some of Louise's clichés a little
(without freshening them too much, for otherwise one of her
characteristic techniques, namely the revelation of the naked
emotion out of its wrapping of stock phrases, could not be
conveyed). I have used a fairly free sonnet-form, in that many
of my rimes are various sorts of approximation. And I have to
some extent borne in mind the sort of poetry being written in
sixteenth-century English by some of Louise's contemporaries. Finally, as with all translations from a regular French
form into a regular English one, a conscientiously literal
translation will often provide one with too few words to fill
the line! For English words are quite simply shorter than
French ones. The occasional addition and interpolation is
unavoidable.   G.D.M.

Louise Labé

>   cupis nomen scire? Loysa fui.
> Non obii, ast abii: nam fama aeterna loquetur,
> Exegi vitae quae monimenta meae.

> Do you want to know my name? I was called Louise.
> I haven't died, I've gone away;
> My undying reputation will tell you
> The lasting achievements of my life.

NICOLAS BOURBON
   Loysae Francisci regis matris epitaphion.

Louise Labé
Sonnets

INTRODUCTION

Louise Labé will always remain something of a mysterious person. On the one hand, we have the slight volume of her works which has a more or less direct impact on the reader, ensuring that she will always be counted among the moderns, and on the other there are the legends which have grown up about her life and loves. Somewhere in between there are the tantalizingly few facts about her which are both certain and significant.

Because of this modernity and universality—which makes Giudici compare her to Leopardi and Kupisz to Mickiewicz —we are tempted to read her poetry as though it was unnecessary to know anything about the times in which she lived; soon, however, we see the impossibility of this since part of the appeal of the sonnet is due to the subtle play between its originality and the tradition out of which it springs. When we first realize the importance of the fact that these love-poems were written by a woman we are very near to appreciating how important it is that it was this woman who wrote them.

The study of the facts of Louise's life seems to have exercised scholars more than her poetry itself has done. It is not possible here to treat all the problems which have been discussed at great length elsewhere, though I shall allude briefly to some of them. Critics are still not agreed about the date of her birth, and until we discover her *acte de naissance*, then I am afraid that we must continue to admit our ignorance. Without a minute analysis of all the arguments (some of which are spurious, others merely circumstantial) we can do no better than to say that she was born about 1520. The

insufficiency of our information on this point is symptomatic
of our ignorance about the rest of her life. An excellent
statement of this comes in one of the detailed and weighty
studies which Enzo Giudici has devoted to her:

> Everything in the life of Louise is uncertain: the nature
> and the circumstances of her education (which was,
> nevertheless, of the first order, and therefore surpri-
> singly above her own social class); what sort of teachers
> she had (and there is no justification for mentioning the
> name of Scève); what her true admirers were like, and
> who were casual ones, what her morals were (Pontus de
> Tyard said she was angelic, Calvin called her *plebeia mere-
> trix* [common whore]), and what was the nature of her
> loves.[1]

We should also take into account that much of what is given
as certain biographical fact often has its sole source in her
poems themselves. Louise Labé was born in Lyon (a city
which because of its geographical position became important
for trade, and especially printing, and so helped to spread the
influence of Italy in France) into a newly rich family, the fifth
child of a rope-maker, Pierre Labé (or Charly) and Etien-
nette Compagnon, a widow and his second wife. Her education
was liberal: it seems certain that she knew Latin and Italian,
with perhaps a smattering of Greek and Spanish, that she had
some musical training and was taught to ride. There is no real
evidence that her tutor was either of the poets Clément
Marot or Maurice Scève as is often thought. We have very
little information about her love life. In one of the *Escriz de
divers poëtes, à la louenge de Louize Labé Lionnoize*, printed in
the original edition after her own poems, there is mention of a
'bon Poëte Rommain', and of a 'homme de guerre'. Now in
spite of some ingenious but dissatisfying crossword-puzzle
solving by Luc van Brabant and his discovery of halting and
recondite anagrams contained mainly in the poetry of Olivier
de Magny, there does not seem sufficient reason to equate
these supposed lovers with Clément Marot and the future
Henri II. (In 1542 Henri was present at the siege of Perpignan
and legend has it that Louise fought there as the Capitaine
Loys, but it seems certain that the most she did was to take
part in some tournaments associated with the siege). About
1544 she married Ennemond Perrin, a rich rope-maker who

was over thirty years older than she. It was a strange marriage which seems to have left her almost total freedom, freedom in particular to run some sort of a literary salon or to invite men of letters to her house.

On 13 March 1554 (old style) she received royal permission to publish her book of poems which appeared in the course of 1555. The book contained twenty-four sonnets, one of which was in Italian, three elegies and a prose dialogue, *Le débat de folie et d'amour*. As well as her own works there are in this book twenty-four poems in her honour composed by other people, in Greek, Latin, Italian and French; we do not know the authorship of all of them though some seem to be correctly attributed to Scève, Baïf, Olivier de Magny and Pontus de Tyard. Olivier de Magny is usually considered to have been the lover whose presence in the sonnets of Louise Labé is most certain. It has been suggested that his last two books of *Odes* refer clearly to her; furthermore there are eight lines of one of Louise's sonnets which are the same as eight lines of one by Magny, and it is also true that, whatever may have been the relationship between the two writers, it seems to have been intense enough for Magny to write in her praise and then later, apparently out of revenge at her rejection of him, to write a vicious attack, treating her as a courtesan.

Louise Labé died more or less forgotten in 1566, shortly after the death of her husband. Her beautiful and ornate tombstone has been lost, so that we do not have that epitaph. The one which most people remember is Calvin's 'plebeia meretrix' of 1561. If her critics were really summoned to be the jurors which they often see themselves as, there would be little danger of arriving at a unanimous decision. I do not wish to enter into the discussion, because it does not have much to do with literary criticism or with our appreciation of the poems. I would just say that Calvin's judgment does not appear to have been based on any actual evidence, and that he was not noted for his tolerance in this matter.

Louise Labé has often been called 'la Sappho lyonnaise'; the first time her name was linked with Sappho's was in the Greek poem published in the *Escriz de divers poëtes*, accompanying her works. She herself says, in the first *Élégie*, (ll.14-16):

Il [sc. Phebus] m'a donné la lyre, qui les vers

Souloit chanter de l'Amour Lesbienne:
Et à ce coup pleurera de la mienne.

[He (sc. Phœbus) gave me the lyre, which used to sing poems of Sapphic love, and will now make lament for mine.]

There are indeed many points of comparison, the main one being that in both cases we have passionately sensual love-poetry written by a woman. It is almost certain, however, that Louise did not know anything of Sappho's poetry either in Greek or in translation. In writing about Louise I shall not follow the example of a writer on Sappho who began his work by saying that she was the greatest artist of all time. I hope that the stress I lay on her artistry does not seem excessive, and that it will appear that this skill of hers in no way detracts from the spontaneity and freshness of her writing, but I do not wish to claim perfection for her. (Sixteenth-century writers were fond of debating whether it was possible to find a perfect grammarian, orator, logician, doctor, courtier, poet and so on.) Some of the sonnets are less polished than the others, some even totally devoid of feeling, and merely part of a common tradition.

Nor will I follow the same writer on Sappho who lays all the distasteful utterances which have been made about Sappho at the door of some other poor girl, a prostitute given to perversion and poetry, who happened also to have been called Sappho. As far as I know there is only one Louise Labé; with many different names (reputation, nom, nomen). Perhaps the principal difference between her and Sappho is that, although we do not know much more about her life than we do about Sappho's, we have far more of her poetry and there is not the same doubt about the text.

Louise Labé's poems possess a freshness and immediacy of appeal, and yet, if we are to appreciate their full force and resonance we must see them against the background of the times during which she lived, try to assess how original they are, and see what effect they would have had on the sixteenth-century reader. It is for this reason that the present commentary pays so much attention to details of language. Furthermore, however spontaneous Louise Labé appears to us now, and even appeared to her contemporaries, we must not forget that she was writing within a tradition, in a climate of writing with characteristics admitting of fairly easy description. Nor must we forget that during the Renaissance the concept of literary and artistic imitation was one which was highly esteemed.

The early 1550s, when Louise Labé was preparing her collection of sonnets, was one of the most important moments in the history of French poetry. It was the time when the group of poets known as the Pléiade, especially Ronsard and Du Bellay, were composing and publishing their early works, developing a theory of poetry, and mastering new techniques. The writing of poetry had never been abandoned in France, but at the end of the fifteenth and the beginning of the sixteenth century, generally speaking, artistic excellence had crystallized and degenerated into verbal juggling in the verse of the Rhétoriqueurs. In the years immediately preceding the first poems by the members of the Pléiade, there were, of course, major works written by other poets, especially Marot and Scève, but the Pléiade at least had the feeling that they were breaking new ground. In 1549, in the *Deffence et illustration de la langue françoyse* Du Bellay appealed to his compatriots to start to compose 'une nouvelle poésie'. His book is important for what he says about the need to look carefully at the rich resources of the French language (as opposed to Latin and Italian), and for his account of the theory of poetic imitation.

It is in this context that the Pléiade composed their first love-poetry. They were consciously attempting to imitate classical and Italian authors and to transfer their beautiful conceptions and expressions into French. There is small wonder that the first love-poems they wrote owed so much to Plato's theory of love, and to Petrarch's *Canzoniere*. In order to understand fully the poems which Louise Labé published in 1555 we must look closer at these two important influences on French love-poetry, Platonism and Petrarchism.

To take Platonism first: there had, of course, been a lively Neo-platonist side to medieval thought, and the study of Plato, in some form or other, had never completely been given up, but at the time of the rediscovery of so much else in classical literature Plato acquired a new and increased popularity: he seemed richer and more rewarding than Aristotle, who was seen as the prime mover of the aridities of the schoolmen. Plato was posthumously converted to Christianity, and baptised by Marsilio Ficino (1433–99); Ficino's commentaries on Plato became a source-book and inspiration for the French poets of the 1550s.

At the same time as the body of Plato's writings was being published in Greek, and in Latin and vernacular translations, his ideas were being popularised in commentaries and other derivative works. The two ways in which this affected literature were (i) there was an attempt to arrive at a new understanding of the nature of poetry and (ii) there was a new conception of the theory of love. These two ideas were closely linked by the writers of the time. One very important work which shows a strong Platonist influence is *La parfaicte amye* of Antoine Héroët (1492(?)–1568, later Bishop of Digne), published in Lyon by Etienne Dolet in 1542, together with a translation-adaptation (written in 1536) of the part of Plato's *Symposium* which contains the myth of the Androgyne. In 1544 the Lyonnais poet Maurice Scève published his *Délie, object de plus haulte vertu*, a poem of 449 dizains, which gives evidence at least of a good knowledge of Plato, and contains some Platonic elements.

Plato's *Ion* was translated into French and published in 1546, and it is mainly from this work that the Platonic elements in the theory of poetry came. Two years later Sebillet begins his *Art poétique françoys*, with a clear account of the Platonic theory of poetry. From 1549 there appear in Paris collections of poems by Ronsard and Du Bellay which owe much to this new way of looking at Plato. In 1552 Pontus de Tyard (who had already published some Platonist love-poetry in his *Erreurs amoureuses*) brought out in Lyon his *Solitaire premier* which is a long description of the same Platonic theories of poetry and of love. It contains especially an account of the four kinds of fury: poetic (coming from the muses), mysterious or priestly (coming from Bacchus), prophetic (coming from Apollo), and amorous (coming from Venus).

The main Platonic themes and images to be found in these poems of the 1540s and 1550s are: the ladder by means of which the lover ascends from the appreciation of physical beauty in a person, to love of the Beautiful and the Good, the contrast between the real and the ideal world, the imprisonment of the soul in the body, the use of the Androgyne myth;

at the same time, there was often an attempt, sometimes super-ficial and half-hearted, to reconcile this mythology with Christian thought.

We must now leave the Platonic elements in sixteenth-century French poetry and turn to the parallel influence exercised by Petrarch and his followers. Here again, the story has been told many times; I wish merely to trace the outlines of it, and show that after the initial excitement brought about by the rediscovery of Petrarch, there set in by 1555, the date of the publication of Louise Labé's sonnets, a deep dissatisfaction with Petrarch as a model for poetic inspira-tion. Petrarch was naturally more accessible to the French poets than was Plato, especially because of the increasing Italian influence on French literature during and after the Italian wars. It was from Petrarch and his successors that the sonnet came into France in the 1540s. There is no need here to go into the question of which of the several claimants was the first to introduce the sonnet.

Among the first French sonnetteers, but on a small scale, were Marot, Mellin de St Gelais and Peletier du Mans. Petrarch's works were translated into French by Vasquin Philieul: in 1548 the first book of *Laure d'Avignon* (196 poems translated), and in 1555 the *Œuvres vulgaires de Françoys Pétrarque* (four books). It is enough to say that from about 1540 onwards there was feverish interest in Petrarch. Scève's *Délie*, for example, which is written in *dizains*, not sonnet-form, owes much more to Petrarch than it does to Plato. The real Petrarchans, how-ever, are Du Bellay and Ronsard. In the same year as he was calling for 'une nouvelle poésie', Du Bellay produced his own first contribution to it, a book of fifty sonnets called *L'Olive*, which was enlarged in 1550 to include one hundred and fifteen sonnets. This is the first Petrarchan sonnet-sequence in French, and is constructed with great craftsmanship; its adaptations are more than competent, capturing the spirit of the original in a French form which is not too rigid. The con-ception of love which it proposes is one in which the woman remains on a pedestal, spiritual and inaccessible; the language of love is often violent, yet is stilted because the poems pro-ceed by antitheses; and the physical and spiritual suffering of love is analyzed. There is a continual play between nature and the condition of the poet-lover in his solitude. It does not matter whether Olive was a real person or not; in any case, however 'sincere' these sonnets may be, they are certainly not spontaneous, direct or passionate. In 1552 Ronsard took up the challenge which Du Bellay had laid down, and published his *Amours*. There we find again much that we had seen in *L'Olive*, and more besides. Ronsard's mastery and learning is greater, and his vision is broader. He still describes Cassandre as inaccessible, but he also includes some poems of physical description (which scandalized Muret, his teacher and commentator). Even though we are fairly well informed about the real Cassandre we somehow still feel that Ronsard is more concerned with making poetry (ποίησις) than with making love. In 1553 he published a short book of *Folastries*, in which he delights in detailed sexual description and playful erotic fantasy. This is worthy of note because the 'real' Ronsard is perhaps the sensual love-poet, not the praiser of elevating spiritual love. The existence of the *Folastries* shows, too, the artificiality of the purely Platonist and Petrarchan poems.

Although Du Bellay, for his part, had brought out (in 1552) thirteen mainly Platonist *Sonnetz de l'honneste amour*, in 1553 he published a poem 'A une dame'[2] which utterly repudiates all writing in the Petrarchan vein. This is worth quoting at some length. I want to show that what Du Bellay does with great sound and fury, Louise Labé does, in fact, more gently, more directly, and less self-consciously, while at the same time keeping many of the stock Petrarchan images and expressions. The poem begins:

> J'ay oublié l'art de petrarquizer.
> Je veux d'amour franchement deviser
> Sans vous flater, et sans me deguiser.
> Ceulx qui font tant de plaintes
> N'ont pas le quart d'une vraye amytié,
> Et n'ont pas tant de peine la moitié,
> Comme leurs yeulx, pour vous faire pitié,
> Getent de larmes faintes.
>
> [I have forgotten the art of petrarchizing. I want to talk frankly of love without flattering you, and without putting on a disguise. Those who make so many laments have not the fourth part of a true friendship, and do not suffer half as much sorrow as their eyes, to arouse your pity, shed feigned tears.]

It continues by giving in an exaggerated fashion all the traditional epithets, and does this in a Petrarchan structure of lists, parallels, antitheses and negations. In ll.73–80 Du Bellay sums this up:

> Mais cet enfer de vaines passions,
> Ce paradis de belles fictions,
> Deguisement de noz affections,
> Ce sont peinctures vaines:
> Qui donnent plus de plaisir aux lisans
> Que voz beautez à tous voz courtisans,
> Et qu'au plus fol de tous ces biendisans
> Vous me donnez de peines.

[But this hell of empty passions, this paradise of beautiful fictions, this disguising of our affections, are all empty pictures, which give more pleasure to their readers than your beauty gives to your suitors, more pleasure than you give sorrow to me, the most infatuated of all your adulators.]

He attacks the romantic appeal to 'antres et fontaines' and to 'solitaires lieux', and goes on (ll.133–6):

> Mais quant à moy, qui plus terrestre suis,
> Et n'aime rien, que ce qu'aimer je puis,
> Le plus subtil, qu'en amour je poursuis,
> S'appelle jouyssance.

[But as for me, who am more down-to-earth, and love nothing but what I *can* love, the greatest subtlety I seek in love is called enjoyment.]

A few lines later (ll.145–52) Du Bellay attacks the use of the myth of Androgyne, and in the next two stanzas he describes the difference between the experience of love and its expression in love-poetry. In ll.153–60 he continues:

> Noz bons ayeux, qui cet art demenoient,
> Pour en causer, Petrarque n'apprenoient,
> Ains franchement leur dame entretenoient
> Sans fard ou couverture.
> Mais aussi tost qu'Amour s'est fait sçavant,
> Lui qui estoit François au paravant,
> Est devenu menteur et decevant,
> Et de Thusque nature.

[Our worthy ancestors, who practised this art, didn't have to learn Petrarch in order to discuss it, but dealt frankly

with their lady without adornment or deceit. But the
moment Love became sophisticated, he ceased to be a
Frenchman, and became a deceitful lying Italian.]

I quote this poem of Du Bellay at such length here because it
seems to me that Du Bellay's initial imitation of Petrarch and
his subsequent rejection of him at exactly the time when
Louise Labé was writing can help us very much in our
appreciation of her poetry.

Ronsard, too, in 1555 rejects both Platonism and Petrarchism
in his *Continuation des amours* which are supposed to be addressed mainly to a peasant girl called Marie. These sonnets are
fresh and sensual (there is much more physical description
than in the sonnets to Cassandre). In his *Élégie à son livre*
(published in 1560 in the second book of *Amours*)[3] in justifying
his rejection of Cassandre he says that he does not believe
Petrarch was chaste and faithful to Laura for thirty-one years:

Ou bien il jouissait de sa Laurette, ou bien
Il estoit un grand fat d'aymer sans avoir rien,
Ce que je ne puis croire, aussi n'est-il croiable.
    (ll.49–51).

[Either he enjoyed his little Laura, or else he was a silly
fool to love and have nothing in return; which I can't
credit, in fact it's not credible.]

Later in the same poem he talks about the simple style necessary for love-poetry:

Les amours ne se souspirent pas
D'un vers hautement grave, ains d'un beau stille bas,
Populaire et plaisant, ainsi qu'a fait Tibulle,
L'ingenieux Ovide, et le docte Catulle:
Le fils de Venus hait ces ostentations:
Il sufist qu'on luy chante au vray ses passions,
Sans enfleure ny fard, d'un mignard et dous stille,
Coulant d'un petit bruit comme une eau qui distille.
    (ll.173–80)

[Love is not sighed out in high-flown serious poetry but in
a fine humble style, popular and pleasing like that of Tibul-
lus, inventive Ovid and learned Catullus; the son of Venus
hates such ostentation: to sing one's passion truthfully is
enough for him, without adornment or exaggeration, and in
a sweet and gentle style flowing softly like water.]

Ronsard was aware of the criticism other people were

making of his poetry, and realized that his craftsmanship was becoming more obvious than his inspiration, that his art was tending to dominate over his natural poetic spontaneity. In the *Odes amoureuses* (1559), Magny carries even further this idea of 'naturalness' by referring it to the experience of love itself, and not just to writing about love. In Ode XI, 'D'aymer en plusieurs lieux, à Guillaume Aubert,' we read:

> Pource qu'en ceste Amour diversement escripte
> Je parle ore avec Anne, ore avec Marguerite,
> Magdaleine, et Loyse, on me pourroit blasmer
> D'aymer en trop de lieux pour bien me faire aymer.
> (ll.1–4)

Magny then goes on to say that he wants to describe these affairs 'naifvement', but says he is incapable of restricting his love to one woman:

> Je suis donq' naturel, et ma felicité
> En matiere d'amour c'est la diversité.
> (ll.15–16)

[For speaking now with Anne, and now with Marguerite, Magdaleine or Louise in this variously dedicated tale of love, I could be blamed for loving in too many places to obtain love in return; I am therefore natural, and my happiness in love lies in variety.]

This account of the love-poetry which immediately preceded the publication of Louise Labé's *Œuvres* in 1555 was essential in order to see how she fits into the tradition and rejection of the tradition. I do not feel that it is fruitful to go into the intricate question of her sources. It is certain that she had some acquaintance with Sannazaro, Marot, Pontus de Tyard, Du Bellay, Ronsard and perhaps Jean Second: there are fairly clear echoes of these poets in her writing. I feel sure, too, that she knew Philieul's translation of Petrarch. Having said this we might give a lengthy list of French, Italian, classical and Neo-Latin authors who can be seen as possible sources. Giudici lists over thirty of these before concluding that most of them amount to no more than tenuous and vague analogies which do not detract in any way from her originality.[4] If we had to assess exactly her debt to tradition we could do no more than to point to the one or two poems, or parts of poems, which seem to be directly imitated or translated; after that we would be left with phrases and images which could have come from a host of writers. It is significant that Louise Labé omits or touches lightly much of what Du Bellay had castigated in his poem and omits many other stock elements which he does not mention. We do not find, for example, the list of negative phrases often found in Petrarchan poetry (e.g. Ronsard, *Amours*, s.49, 'Ni de son chef le tresor crépelu'). Nor do we find an analysis of the traditional conflict between love and reason (e.g. Ronsard, *Amours*, s.69, ll.5–6),

> Amour adonc qui sape, mine et ronge
> De ma raison le chancelant rempart,
>
> [Love therefore which saps, undermines and digs away
> beneath the tottering rampart of my reason.]

or the frequent lists of *adynata*, or impossible events, (e.g. Baïf, *Amours de Francine*, I, s.103).

Furthermore, some of the Petrarchan techniques in her writing are little more than the equivalent of the ready-made words and phrases in which we try to convey our emotions. Many of these techniques go back far beyond Petrarch, and are part of the literary language of love in Western Europe from earliest times.

Critics have pointed to specific differences between the two traditions (Platonism and Petrarchism) in the writing of love-poetry:[5] that there is no room for jealousy in the Platonist conception of love, and that there is a different notion of virtue (moral as opposed to the courtly elegance of the Petrarchan ideal); that Platonic love is reciprocal rather than one-sided, and that the chastity of the Petrarchans was reluctant whereas that of the Platonists was something to be striven for. These differences should be borne in mind when attempting to site Louise Labé in the tradition.

Everyone agrees that Louise Labé's poetry is sincere, spontaneous and passionate. This does not, however, mean only that it expresses directly her own personal passionate experience, but rather that it creates a new one which is independent of the lived experience. It is noteworthy that this effect is achieved, for the most part, without any physical description of the lover; there is very little of the traditional description such as Ronsard's

> Ces liens d'or, ceste bouche vermeille,
> Pleine de lis, de roses, et d'œuilletz . . .
>   (*Amours*, s.6, ll.1–2),

[These golden bonds, those carmine lips, full of lilies, roses and carnations.]

and nothing at all like Ronsard's

> Je vouldroy bien richement jaunissant
> En pluye d'or goute à goute descendre
> Dans le beau sein de ma belle Cassandre,
> Lors qu'en ses yeulx le somme va glissant.
>
> (*Amours*, s.20, ll.1–4),

[Turning to a rich rain of gold, drop by drop I want to flow into the lovely bosom of my beautiful Cassandre, when drowsiness swims into her eyes.]

to say nothing of the sexual description in some of his *Folastries*. Nor do we find the physical directness of Magny's *Gayetez* (1554), for example, poem *71*, 'A s'Amie' which begins 'Ma mignarde Nymfelette' and ends by suggesting (though not describing) the 'cinquième point', or of the *Odes amoureuses* (1559) where Ode XLII is 'Description d'une nuict amoureuse' and Ode XLIII is 'Sur ce mesme propos'.

Her sensual writing is of a different kind altogether. She is sparing of images, especially of classical images and conceits. Her language, too, is usually less artificial than that of many of her contemporaries. Her writing is not full of neologism, she does not use Latin and Greek words as profusely as others did, she uses few diminutives and does not have the verbal inventiveness of Scève and Ronsard, who frequently formed new words by altering parts of speech (infinitives as nouns, adjectives for adverbs, new adverbs in '-ment' and so on). Nor does she have the dense syntactic inventiveness of Scève.

In the course of my commentary I shall give the impression that her sonnet-sequence has some kind of structure. It is generally agreed now that there is not a linear development. Bernard Jourdain even goes so far as to say, 'L'anecdote n'est à peu près rien, et l'ordre des sonnets, comme des élégies, paraît interchangeable'[6] [The story is scarcely important at all, and the order of the sonnets, as of the elegies, seems interchangeable'.] There is, indeed, very little story. I am not sure, however, to what extent the order could be rearranged without an alteration of the total effect (especially with reference to the relative positions of the sensual, the mythological and the trite Petrarchan sonnets).

There is no sense in trying to relate the poems directly to

Louise's lived experience. It is, of course, hard to believe that they are *not* based on personal experience, and if they are not, then obviously the achievement is greater. What concerns us, however, are the poems themselves, and here, it must be noted, there are different degrees of reality, and different times or periods (though the precise chronology is not made clear). In the first *Élégie* Louise writes:

> Je sen desja un piteus souvenir
> Qui me contreint la larme à l'œil venir.
>
> [A heartbreaking memory now comes to me, bringing tears to my eyes.]

Memory plays a large part in the sonnets, even if it is only within the *created* experience. The second and third *Élégies*, especially, contain some narrative: the second one is a letter to a lover who is absent, and whom she reproaches with infidelity ('As tu si peu de memoire de moy,/Que de m'avoir si tot rompu la foy?' ll.11–12) [Have you so little memory of me that you have broken faith with me so soon?], and the third seems to contain an autobiographical reference:

> Je n'avois vù encore seize Hivers,
> Lors que j'entray en ces ennuis divers:
> Et jà voici le treiziéme Esté
> Que mon cœur fut par Amour arresté.
>   (ll.73–76)
>
> [I had not yet seen sixteen winters, when I first encountered these different troubles, and now it is the thirteenth summer since Love captured my heart.]

So it is that s.14 (l.2) can say 'A l'heur passé avec toy regretter', and *Élégie* II 'Ores je croy, vù notre amour passee,/Qu'impossible est, que tu m'aies laissee:' (ll.27–8) [Now I think, in view of our past love, that it's impossible you have left me.]

In the *Epître dédicatoire* she defines thus the rôle of memory in her writing:

> Car le passé nous resjouit, et sert plus que le present: mais les plaisirs des sentimens se perdent incontinent, et ne reviennent jamais, et en est quelquefois la memoire autant facheuse, comme les actes ont esté delectables. Davantage les autres voluptez sont telles, que quelque souvenir qui en vienne, si ne nous peut il remettre en telle disposicion que nous estions: et quelque imaginacion forte que nous

imprimions en la teste, si connoissons nous bien que ce n'est qu'une ombre du passé qui nous abuse et trompe. Mais quand il avient que mettons par escrit nos concepcions combien que puis apres notre cerveau coure par une infinite d'afaires et incessamment remue, si est ce que long tems apres reprenans nos escrits, nous revenons au mesme point, et à la mesme disposicion ou nous estions. Lors nous redouble notre aise : car nous retrouvons le plaisir passé qu'avons ù en la matiere dont escrivions, ou en l'intelligence des sciences ou lors estions adonnez. Et outre ce, le jugement que font nos secondes concepcions des premieres, nous rend un singulier contentement. [For the past delights us, and is of more service to us than the present; but the pleasures of our senses vanish immediately, never to return, and sometimes our memory of them is as troublesome as the acts themselves were delightful. Moreover the other pleasures are such that, whatever recollection of them comes to us, it cannot return us to our original state, and however vivid the image of it we fix in our minds, we know well that it is only a shadow of the past deceiving and beguiling us. But when it happens that we set down our ideas in writing, though afterwards our minds are occupied by an infinity of matters and kept unceasingly in movement, yet if we take up what we have written a long time afterwards, we come back to the same point, and the same state we were in before. Then our enjoyment is doubled : for we rediscover the past pleasure we had in the experience we wrote about, or in the understanding of the subjects which we were then devoted to. Besides, the comparison between our earlier feelings and our later ones gives us extraordinary pleasure.]

She goes on to say that she had written 'ces jeunesses' as 'un honneste passetems et moyen de fuir oisiveté', and later published them at the insistence of her friends. In *Le débat* she says 'Brief, le plus grand plaisir qui soit apres amour, c'est d'en parler'. [In short, the greatest pleasure after love, in speaking of it.]

In spite of some references to God and the soul in her poetry, love, for Louise Labé, remains an utterly human experience. In the words of Giudici:

The continual contrast between heaven and earth, between

spirit and flesh, which runs through all Petrarch's poetry, is cancelled out in that of Louise.[7]

Giudici says also that her egoism or selfishness is cosmic:

> On the wings of hope and desire, Louise becomes intoxica-
> ted with light; she is selfish, yes, but with an egoism which
> extends to the whole universe; she is free, and for her, life
> is only *her* life, but she can say this without lowering her-
> self, because she has filled her own living with the greatest
> significance of Being.[8]

This kind of criticism will not appeal to an English reader (as Harvey's analyses of structure did not appeal to Giudici), but at least we can take the point that love, for Louise, is essentially pagan love, the *eros* of the Greeks, absolute selfishness as a good and desirable quality. Giudici himself sums this up when he says elsewhere:

> The sensuality of Louise is one with her spirituality; body
> and soul, spirit and flesh are not for her, as for the medieval
> mystics, contrasting entities, but, according to the spirit
> of the Renaissance, aspects of one and the same reality.[9]

He goes on to talk of her innocence, 'because to the pure all things are pure'. It is for the same reason that Louise herself, in *Élégie* III (ll.5–7) says:

> Ne veuillez point condamner ma simplesse,
> Et jeune erreur de ma fole jeunesse,
> Si c'est erreur:
>
> [Please do not condemn my simplicity, and the youthful
> error of my foolish youth— if error it is.]

In a recent article in *The French Review*, Sandy Petrey dis-
cusses 'The Character of the Speaker in the Poetry of Louise
Labé'.[10] The author attempts to say *why* Louise Labé is better
than other minor contemporary poets. He finds the answer in
the profound effects which love has on her personality, beyond
the 'transitory emotional state it produces'. He feels even that
the presence of the lover is not really important. In s.21, for
example, ('Quelle grandeur rend l'homme venerable?') he
sees the question not so much as a device used to bring freshness, but says,

> . . . the interrogative form has the more important result
> of focusing the reader's attention squarely on the speaker
> and denying the lover any existence beyond her attitude
> to him.

In the same way Giudici has noted that the suffering is not so much the result of the insufficiency of love itself, or because of moral and religious tension, but rather that the lover does not correspond to her love, though he does to her ideal.[11]

There is certainly truth in the suggestion that the lover has no existence apart from what she says about him, and that her pain comes from his absence or distance from her. I feel, however, that if we pay too much attention to the absence of the lover we will end up by devaluing the sonnets. As we now turn to the sonnets themselves we shall see the importance of the lover within the created experience.

NOTES

1 Giudici, II, 72; (see bibliography). The translation is my own.
2 Du Bellay *Œuvres poétiques*, ed. H. Chamard (Paris, 1908–31), IV, 205–15.
3 Ronsard, *Les amours*, ed. H. et C. Weber, 251–7.
4 Giudici, I, 102.
5 Cf., especially Saulnier, *Maurice Scève*, I, 207ff.
6 Jourdain, B., *Louise Labé: Élégies, Sonnets, Débat* (Paris, 1953) 16–17.
7 Giudici, I, 98.
8 Ibid., 99.
9 Giudici, II, 288.
10 Vol. XLIII (March 1970) 588–96.
11 Giudici, I, 99–100.

The Sonnets

1) Non hauria Ulysse o qualunqu'altro mai
     Piu accorto fù, da quel divino aspetto
     Pien di gratie, d'honor e di rispetto
     Sperato qual i sento affanni e guai.

     Pur, Amour, co i begli ochi tu fatt' hai
     Tal piaga dentro al mio innocente petto,
     Di cibo e di calor gia tuo ricetto,
     Che rimedio non v'e si tu n'el dai.

     O sorte dura, che mi fa esser quale
     Punta d'un Scorpio, e domandar riparo
     Contr'el velen' dall'istesso animale.

     Chieggio li sol'ancida questa noia,
     Non estingua el desir à me si caro,
     Che mancar non potra ch'i non mi muoia.

2) Ô beaus yeus bruns, ô regars destournez,
     Ô chaus soupirs, ô larmes espandues,
     Ô noires nuits vainement atendues,
     Ô jours luisans vainement retournez:

     Ô tristes pleins, ô desirs obstinez,
     Ô tems perdu, ô peines despendues,
     Ô mile morts en mile rets tendues,
     Ô pires maus contre moi destinez.

     Ô ris, ô front, cheveus, bras, mains et doits:
     Ô lut pleintif, viole, archet et vois:
     Tant de flambeaus pour ardre une femmelle !

     De toy me plein, que tant de feus portant,
     En tant d'endrois d'iceus mon cœur tatant,
     N'en est sur toy volé quelque estincelle.

1) Even a man far wiser than the wise
Odysseus could never have predicted
The many bitter sufferings inflicted
By the sweet gaze of two such handsome eyes.

For, love, you turned their beauty like a blade
Against my innocent breast and made it bleed;
And there you nestle warm, and there you feed;
But you alone can heal the wound you made.

Intolerable fate: for remedy
To this infection forced to supplicate
The very scorpion that poisoned me.

Then please, Love, I implore you, terminate
This agony of mine; but don't dispel
My hot desire, else I should die as well.

2) O handsome eyes, brown eyes, O gaze that's turned
Away, O fervent sighs, tears unabated,
O darkness of the night in vain awaited,
O brightness of the dawn in vain returned!

O obstinate desires, O sad laments,
O wasted time, O labour of regret,
O thousand deaths that bait a thousand nets,
O blackest fate upon my harm hell-bent!

O laughter, forehead, hair, arms, fingers, hands!
O poignant lute, bow, viol, singing voice!
All flames within the furnace that destroys

This one poor woman. Almost I despair;
My heart's a house assailed with flaming brands;
Yet not one spark to catch and make *you* flare.

3) Ô longs desirs, ô esperances vaines,
     Tristes soupirs et larmes coutumieres
     A engendrer de moy maintes rivieres,
     Dont mes deus yeus sont sources et fontaines:

     Ô cruautez, ô durtez inhumaines,
     Piteus regars des celestes lumieres:
     Du cœur transi ô passions premieres,
     Estimez vous croitre encore mes peines ?

     Qu'encor Amour sur moy son arc essaie,
     Que nouveaus feus me gette et nouveaus dars:
     Qu'il se despite, et pis qu'il pourra face:

     Car je suis tant navree en toutes pars,
     Que plus en moy une nouvelle plaie,
     Pour m'empirer ne pourroit trouver place.

4) Depuis qu'Amour cruel empoisonna
     Premierement de son feu ma poitrine,
     Tousjours brulay de sa fureur divine,
     Qui un seul jour mon cœur n'abandonna.

     Quelque travail, dont assez me donna,
     Quelque menasse et procheine ruïne:
     Quelque penser de mort qui tout termine,
     De rien mon cœur ardent ne s'estonna.

     Tant plus qu'Amour nous vient fort assaillir,
     Plus il nous fait nos forces recueillir,
     Et tousjours frais en ses combats fait estre:

     Mais ce n'est pas qu'en rien nous favorise,
     Cil qui les Dieus et les hommes mesprise:
     Mais pour plus fort contre les fors paroitre.

3) O long desire, O futile hope, O sighs
  Of grief and customary tears that cause
  A river of despair to rise, whose source
  And only fountain is my weeping eyes!

  O cruel inhumanities, that tempt
  To heavenly pity all the watching stars,
  O primal passion of the spellbound heart,
  How could you make my sorrow more intense?

  Then with his bow let Love again take aim
  And let his anger flare and do its worst,
  Firing more arrows at me and more flame:

  For now so many are my wounds at last
  How could he find a target there to hurt
  Me more? There's no room left within my heart.

4) Since the first moment when my bosom caught
  The fire of Love's infection, I was prey
  To his divine delirium, that brought
  No respite even for a single day.

  Whatever toils (and they were Herculean),
  Whatever thoughts of death where all thought dies,
  Whatever threats or imminence of ruin,
  None of them could my eager heart surprise.

  The stronger cruel Love comes armed to war,
  The more he puts us on our mettle, more
  Reserves we muster. If you fancy, then,

  He means to give us quarter, you'd be wrong
  —For small respect he shows to gods or men—
  But to be stronger still against the strong.

5) Clere Venus, qui erres par les Cieus,
     Entens ma voix qui en pleins chantera,
     Tant que ta face au haut du Ciel luira,
     Son long travail et souci ennuieus.

     Mon œil veillant s'atendrira bien mieus,
     Et plus de pleurs te voyant getera.
     Mieus mon lit mol de larmes baignera,
     De ses travaus voyant témoins tes yeus.

     Donq des humains sont les lassez esprits
     De dous repos et de sommeil espris.
     J'endure mal tant que le Soleil luit:

     Et quand je suis quasi toute cassee,
     Et que me suis mise en mon lit lassee,
     Crier me faut mon mal toute la nuit.

6) Deus ou trois fois bienheureus le retour
     De ce cler Astre, et plus heureus encore
     Ce que son œil de regarder honore.
     Que celle là recevroit un bon jour,

     Qu'elle pourroit se vanter d'un bon tour
     Qui baiseroit le plus beau don de Flore,
     Le mieus sentant que jamais vid Aurore,
     Et y feroit sur ses levres sejour!

     C'est à moy seule à qui ce bien est du,
     Pour tant de pleurs et tant de tems perdu:
     Mais le voyant, tant lui feray de feste,

     Tant emploiray de mes yeus le pouvoir,
     Pour dessus lui plus de credit avoir,
     Qu'en peu de tems feray grande conqueste.

5) Bright Venus, who across the heavens stray,
　　I pray you be my listener and witness;
　　My voice, while still your star is shining high,
　　Will bitterly lament its loving sickness.

　　My waking eye will melt more readily
　　When you are there to see, more tears will shed
　　Seeing your watching eye, more easily
　　Sorrow to weeping brims and soaks my bed.

　　Now human souls are all in love with sleep,
　　In gentle resting, restoration seek.
　　Too long the sunlight, pitiless and strong;

　　And when my heart is brought almost to breaking,
　　Then I to bed, lonely and tired of waking,
　　Retire and cry my pain out all night long.

6) Twice or thrice happy is the rising light
　　Of that returning Star, and happier still
　　Everything that is honoured by his bright
　　And shining gaze. What a good morning will

　　Greet her when Flora offers her to pluck
　　The sweetest scented flower Dawn can glimpse;
　　O then how she will think herself in luck
　　To kiss that flower and dwell upon his lips!

　　This recompense is mine, to me is owing
　　For long expense of time and waste of tears;
　　But seeing him, with welcome overflowing

　　I'll so employ the power of my gaze
　　I'll gain more credit, his defences pierce
　　And make great conquest in a little space.

7) On voit mourir toute chose animee,
     Lors que du corps l'ame sutile part:
     Je suis le corps, toy la meilleure part:
     Ou es-tu donq, ô ame bien aymee ?

     Ne me laissez par si long tems pámee,
     Pour me sauver apres viendrois trop tard.
     Las, ne mets point ton corps en ce hazart:
     Ren lui sa part et moitié estimee.

     Mais fais, Ami, que ne soit dangereuse
     Cette rencontre et revuë amoureuse,
     L'acompagnant, non de severité,

     Non de rigueur: mais de grace amiable,
     Qui doucement me rende ta beauté,
     Jadis cruelle, à present favorable.

8) Je vis, je meurs: je me brule et me noye.
     J'ay chaut estreme en endurant froidure:
     La vie m'est et trop molle et trop dure.
     J'ay grans ennuis entremeslez de joye:

     Tout à un coup je ris et je larmoye,
     Et en plaisir maint grief tourment j'endure:
     Mon bien s'en va, et à jamais il dure:
     Tout en un coup je seiche et je verdoye.

     Ainsi Amour inconstamment me meine:
     Et quand je pense avoir plus de douleur,
     Sans y penser je me treuve hors de peine.

     Puis quand je croy ma joye estre certeine,
     Et estre au haut de mon desiré heur,
     Il me remet en mon premier malheur.

7) When soul from body like fine smoke departs
    Then every living thing to death must go:
    I am the body, you its better part:
    Where are you then, my well-beloved soul?

    Do not abandon me so long to swoon
    For saving of my life you'd come too late.
    Do not imperil your own body: soon
    Return to it, restore and animate.

    And, love, do not permit our amorous
    Reunion to be hard and hazardous;
    So with no rigour let it be combined

    And with no harshness, but with friendly duty
    Gently restoring to me all your beauty,
    So long so cruel, now at last so kind.

8) I live and die; drowning I burn to death,
    Seared by the ice and frozen by the fire;
    Life is as hard as iron, as soft as breath;
    My joy and trouble dance on the same wire.

    In the same sudden breath I laugh and weep,
    My torment pleasure where my pleasure grieves;
    My treasure's lost which I for all time keep,
    At once I wither and put out new leaves.

    Thus constant Love is my inconstant guide;
    And when I am to pain's refinement brought,
    Beyond all hope, he grants me a reprieve.

    And when I think joy cannot be denied,
    And scaled the peak of happiness I sought,
    He casts me down into my former grief.

9) Tout aussi tot que je commence à prendre
     Dens le mol lit le repos desiré,
     Mon triste esprit hors de moy retiré
     S'en va vers toy incontinent se rendre.

     Lors m'est avis que dedens mon sein tendre
     Je tiens le bien, ou j'ay tant aspiré,
     Et pour lequel j'ay si haut souspiré,
     Que de sanglots ay souvent cuidé fendre.

     Ô dous sommeil, ô nuit à moy heureuse !
     Plaisant repos, plein de tranquilité,
     Continuez toutes les nuiz mon songe :

     Et si jamais ma povre ame amoureuse
     Ne doit avoir de bien en verité,
     Faites au moins qu'elle en ait en mensonge.

10) Quand j'aperçoy ton blond chef couronné
      D'un laurier verd, faire un Lut si bien pleindre,
      Que tu pourrois à te suivre contreindre
      Arbres et rocs : quand je te vois orné,

      Et de vertus dix mile environné,
      Au chef d'honneur plus haut que nul ateindre,
      Et des plus hauts les louenges esteindre :
      Lors dit mon cœur en soy passionné :

      Tant de vertus qui te font estre aymé,
      Qui de chacun te font estre estimé,
      Ne te pourroient aussi bien faire aymer ?

      Et ajoutant à ta vertu louable
      Ce nom encor de m'estre pitoyable,
      De mon amour doucement t'enflamer ?

9) No sooner does my bed softly induce
    Me to the sweet repose for which I long,
    The spirit from my body breaking loose
    On wings of sorrow flies to you headlong.

    Then I imagine fondly to my side
    I press that dearest treasure for whose sake
    So many bitter tears I have cried,
    So often thought my body like to break

    In two. O sleep, O respite of delight,
    O pleasant rest and peaceful, I enjoin
    You to repeat this same dream every night;

    And if it's destiny's intent to cheat
    And dispossess my soul of love's true coin,
    At least let me receive love's counterfeit.

10) When I perceive your fair head crowned with laurel,
    And listen as you make the lute-strings grieve
    So plaintively you almost might compel
    The trees and rocks to follow you; perceive

    How people give you honour's rank, and rate
    Your tale of virtues higher than ten thousand,
    So you by greater praise eclipse the great,
    Why then my heart begins to ask, impassioned:

    'Seeing that everyone is moved to love
    And prize your excellence, you surely could
    By that same excellence to love be moved?

    And adding one more to your multitude
    Of virtues—that of pity for my plight—
    At my love's tinder gently catch alight?'

11) Ô dous regars, ô yeus pleins de beauté,
     Petis jardins, pleins de fleurs amoureuses
     Ou sont d'Amour les flesches dangereuses,
     Tant à vous voir mon œil s'est arresté!

     Ô cœur felon, ô rude cruauté,
     Tant tu me tiens de façons rigoureuses,
     Tant j'ay coulé de larmes langoureuses,
     Sentant l'ardeur de mon cœur tourmenté!

     Donques, mes yeus, tant de plaisir avez
     Tant de bons tours par ses yeus recevez:
     Mais toy, mon cœur, plus les vois s'y complaire,

     Plus tu languiz, plus en as de souci,
     Or devinez si je suis aise aussi,
     Sentant mon œil estre à mon cœur contraire.

12) Lut, compagnon de ma calamité,
     De mes soupirs témoin irreprochable,
     De mes ennuis controlleur veritable,
     Tu as souvent avec moy lamenté:

     Et tant le pleur piteus t'a molesté,
     Que commençant quelque son delectable,
     Tu le rendois tout soudein lamentable,
     Feingnant le ton que plein avoit chanté.

     Et si te veus efforcer au contraire,
     Tu te destens et si me contreins taire:
     Mais me voyant tendrement soupirer,

     Donnant faveur à ma tant triste pleinte:
     En mes ennuis me plaire suis contreinte,
     Et d'un dous mal douce fin esperer.

1) O gentle gaze, O eyes where beauty grows,
   Like little gardens full of amorous flowers,
   Where Love lets fly sharp arrows from his bow,
   Where my eyes too have gazed for many an hour.

   O felon heart, O savage cruelty,
   Binding me in so many iron chains,
   So many are my lovesick tears and sighs,
   My heart so tortured by its burning pain.

   Thus you, my eyes, so much delight have had
   From gazing in his eyes, so much enjoyment;
   But you, my heart, the more you see them glad

   The more you languish and the worse your torment.
   Then guess if there is any joy for me,
   Knowing my heart and eyes thus disagree.

2) Lute, in disaster my most loyal friend,
   Unimpeachable witness of my pain,
   With me you've sorrowed time and time again,
   Giving of all my grief a true account;

   By piteous tears you were so often wrung
   That when I meant some sweet concordant sound
   You turned it suddenly to a lament,
   Assumed the tones to which my sorrow sang.

   And if I try to force you into joy,
   Unstrung you check me and my song destroy:
   But when you hear how tender my complaint

   And to my sighs melodiously assent,
   To pleasure in my pain I am constrained
   And hope a grief so sweet may sweetly end.

13) Oh si j'estois en ce beau sein ravie
       De celui là pour lequel vois mourant:
       Si avec lui vivre le demeurant
       De mes cours jours ne m'empeschoit envie:

       Si m'acollant me disoit, chere Amie,
       Contentons nous l'un l'autre, s'asseurant
       Que ja tempeste, Euripe, ne Courant
       Ne nous pourra desjoindre en notre vie:

       Si de mes bras le tenant acollé,
       Comme du Lierre est l'arbre encercelé,
       La mort venoit, de mon aise envieuse:

       Lors que souef plus il me baiseroit,
       Et mon esprit sur ses levres fuiroit,
       Bien je mourrois, plus que vivante, heureuse.

14) Tant que mes yeus pourront larmes espandre,
       A l'heur passé avec toy regretter:
       Et qu'aus sanglots et soupirs resister
       Pourra ma voix, et un peu faire entendre:

       Tant que ma main pourra les cordes tendre
       Du mignart Lut, pour tes graces chanter:
       Tant que l'esprit se voudra contenter
       De ne vouloir rien fors que toy comprendre:

       Je ne souhaitte encore point mourir.
       Mais quand mes yeus je sentiray tarir,
       Ma voix cassee, et ma main impuissante,

       Et mon esprit en ce mortel sejour
       Ne pouvant plus montrer signe d'amante:
       Prirey la Mort noircir mon plus cler jour.

3) If I were gathered up in that embrace
     For lack of which my life resembles dying,
     And if exempt from deadly envy's prying
     I lived with him the rest of my brief days;

     And if embracing me, he said: 'Dear love,
     Let's make each other happy, and forbid
     Anger of storm or Euripus or flood
     Ever to separate us while we live';

     If holding him as ivy clothes the tree,
     My arms enfolding him as sheath the knife,
     And as he gently kissed me, envious death

     Came to devour my gladness, and my breath
     Upon his lips was sucked away, I'd be
     Happier far in death than in my life.

4) While still my eyes have tears to shed, regretting
     How joyful time with you has fled away,
     While still there's power in my wrist to play,
     Your gentleness to gentle music setting,

     While still my voice can find the self-command
     To sing of you, and overcome a sigh,
     While still my soul can other thoughts deny,
     And you are all it seeks to comprehend,

     I shall not yet desire the embrace of death.
     But when I feel the tears dry on my face,
     My voice broken, my hand bereft of strength,

     My spirit in this mortal dwelling-place
     Showing no sign of love, then I shall pray
     Death to efface in night my brightest day.

15)   Pour le retour du Soleil honorer,
       Le Zephir, l'air serein lui apareille:
       Et du sommeil l'eau et la terre esveille,
       Qui les gardoit l'une de murmurer,

       En dous coulant, l'autre de se parer
       De mainte fleur de couleur nompareille.
       Ja les oiseaus es arbres font merveille,
       Et aus passans font l'ennui moderer:

       Les Nynfes ja en mile jeus s'esbatent
       Au cler de Lune, et dansans l'herbe abatent:
       Veus tu Zephir de ton heur me donner,

       Et que par toy toute me renouvelle ?
       Fay mon Soleil devers moy retourner,
       Et tu verras s'il ne me rend plus belle.

16)   Apres qu'un tems la gresle et le tonnerre
       Ont le haut mont de Caucase batu,
       Le beau jour vient, de lueur revétu.
       Quand Phebus ha son cerne fait en terre,

       Et l'Ocean il regaigne à grand erre:
       Sa seur se montre avec son chef pointu.
       Quand quelque tems le Parthe ha combatu,
       Il prent la fuite et son arc il desserre.

       Un tems t'ay vù et consolé pleintif,
       Et defiant de mon feu peu hatif:
       Mais maintenant que tu m'as embrasee,

       Et suis au point auquel tu me voulois:
       Tu as ta flame en quelque eau arrosee,
       Et es plus froit qu'estre je ne soulois.

) To honour the bright Sun at his arising,
   The Zephyr blows, breaking the air's unruffled
   Dream of the night, and urgently arousing
   Both earth and water from their sleep, that muffled

   The murmur of the softly running stream
   And kept the earth from showing off her gay
   Wardrobe of flowers. The early songbirds seem
   To whistle men's anxieties away,

   And in the moonlight nymphs already glide
   In careless play, and dance the grasses flat.
   Then will you, Zephyr, share your joy with me,

   Renew me with your morning breath? Invite
   My Sun to turn towards me: you will see
   That beauty to my beauty he will add.

) Passionately the thunder and the hail
   Besiege awhile the Caucasus' grim heights,
   Then day returns, caparisoned in light.
   When Phœbus has described his curving trail

   Over the land, and plunges to the sea,
   His sister in her pointed head-dress climbs
   The sky. The Parthian battles for a time,
   Then shoots an arrow as he turns to flee.

   When you were sad, I gave you consolation,
   Though my distrustful fire was slow to suasion;
   But now that you have set a flame to me

   And I am at the point of your desire,
   Some water you have found to douse your fire,
   Are colder than I ever used to be.

17)   Je fuis la vile, et temples, et tous lieus,
       Esquels prenant plaisir à t'ouir pleindre,
       Tu peus, et non sans force, me contreindre
       De te donner ce qu'estimois le mieus.

       Masques, tournois, jeus me sont ennuieus,
       Et rien sans toy de beau ne me puis peindre:
       Tant que tachant à ce desir esteindre,
       Et un nouvel obget faire à mes yeus,

       Et des pensers amoureus me distraire,
       Des bois espais sui le plus solitaire:
       Mais j'aperçoy, ayant erré maint tour,

       Que, si je veus de toy estre delivre,
       Il me convient hors de moymesme vivre,
       Ou fais encor que loin sois en sejour.

18)   Baise m'encor, rebaise moy et baise:
       Donne m'en un de tes plus savoureus,
       Donne m'en un de tes plus amoureus:
       Je t'en rendray quatre plus chaus que braise.

       Las, te pleins tu ? ça que ce mal j'apaise,
       En t'en donnant dix autres doucereus.
       Ainsi meslans nos baisers tant heureus
       Jouissons nous l'un de l'autre à notre aise.

       Lors double vie à chacun en suivra.
       Chacun en soy et son ami vivra.
       Permets m'Amour penser quelque folie:

       Tousjours suis mal, vivant discrettement,
       Et ne me puis donner quelque contentement,
       Si hors de moy ne fay quelque saillie.

7) In town and temple I'm no longer seen,
Where I was glad to hear your grief confessed,
Where still you can compel me, with no mean
Force, to surrender what we valued best.

I'm bored with masques and tournaments and games,
I can imagine nothing fine but you,
But I endeavour to put out these flames
And change the old desire for something new.

To take my mind off thoughts of love, I stray
Lonely among the loneliest of trees,
But wander as I may, if I'm to be

Delivered from you, then there is no help
For it: I'll have to live outside myself,
Or you to make your home long miles away.

8) Kiss me again, kiss, kiss me again;
Give me the tastiest you have to give,
Pay me the lovingest you have to spend:
And I'll return you four, hotter than live

Coals. Oh, are you sad? There! I'll ease
The pain with ten more kisses, honey-sweet.
And so kiss into happy kiss will melt,
We'll pleasantly enjoy each other's selves.

Then double life will to us both ensue:
You also live in me, as I in you.
So do not chide me for this play on words

Or keep me staid and stay-at-home, but make me
Go on that journey best of all preferred:
When out of myself, my dearest love, you take me.

19) Diane estant en l'espesseur d'un bois,
      Apres avoir mainte beste assenee,
      Prenoit le frais, de Nynfes couronnee:
      J'allois resvant comme fay maintefois,

      Sans y penser: quand j'ouy une vois,
      Qui m'apela, disant, Nynfe estonnee,
      Que ne t'es tu vers Diane tournee?
      Et me voyant sans arc et sans carquois,

      Qu'as tu trouvé, ô compagne, en ta voye,
      Qui de ton arc et flesches ait fait proye?
      Je m'animay, respons je, à un passant,

      Et lui getay en vain toutes mes flesches
      Et l'arc apres: mais lui les ramassant
      Et les tirant me fit cent et cent bresches.

20) Predit me fut, que devoit fermement
      Un jour aymer celui dont la figure
      Me fut descrite: et sans autre peinture
      Le reconnu quand vy premierement:

      Puis, le voyant aymer fatalement,
      Pitié je pris de sa triste aventure:
      Et tellement je forçay ma nature,
      Qu'autant que lui aymay ardentement.

      Qui n'ust pensé qu'en faveur devoit croitre
      Ce que le Ciel et destins firent naitre?
      Mais quand je voy si nubileus aprets,

      Vents si cruels et tant horrible orage:
      Je croy qu'estoient les infernaus arrets,
      Qui de si loin m'ourdissoient ce naufrage.

19)   Many a stag Diana hunted down
       Among the thickets, then beside a stream
       Rested among her crowd of nymphs, her crown.
       And I went dreaming, as I often dream,

       Unthinking, when a sudden voice addressed
       Me saying, 'Wide-eyed Nymph, the path you're on
       Will never lead you to Diana.' Then,
       Seeing my quiver and my bow were lost,

       'Companion, on your way what did you find
       That stole your weapons from you?' 'I took aim
       At someone passing by me,' I replied.

       'Every last dart I cast and after them
       The bow as well; he picked them from the ground
       And shot; and every arrow made a wound.'

20)   A fortune-teller told me once my fate,
       Described the very man who was to be
       One day my love; I saw no other portrait,
       But when I met him knew him instantly.

       And when I saw his love for me deject
       His spirit, pitied his adversity,
       And forced my feelings to such good effect
       I came to love as fervently as he.

       What was begun by the celestial will
       You would have thought was bound to prosper well,
       But when I see the angry clouds that fill

       The sky, and how Aeolus' winds are freed,
       I think it was by ordinance of Hell
       My shipwreck on this reef was long decreed.

21)   Quelle grandeur rend l'homme venerable?
        Quelle grosseur? quel poil? quelle couleur?
        Qui est des yeus le plus emmieleur?
        Qui fait plus tot une playe incurable?

        Quel chant est plus à l'homme convenable?
        Qui plus penetre en chantant sa douleur?
        Qui un dous lut fait encore meilleur?
        Quel naturel est le plus amiable?

        Je ne voudrois le dire assurément,
        Ayant Amour forcé mon jugement:
        Mais je say bien et de tant je m'assure,

        Que tout le beau que l'on pourroit choisir,
        Et que tout l'art qui ayde la Nature,
        Ne me sauroient acroitre mon desir.

22)   Luisant Soleil, que tu es bien heureus,
        De voir tousjours de t'Amie la face:
        Et toy, sa seur, qu'Endimion embrasse,
        Tant te repais de miel amoureus.

        Mars voit Venus: Mercure aventureus
        De Ciel en Ciel, de lieu en lieu se glasse:
        Et Jupiter remarque en mainte place
        Ses premiers ans plus gays et chaleureus.

        Voilà du Ciel la puissante harmonie,
        Qui les esprits divins ensemble lie:
        Mais, s'ils avoient ce qu'ils ayment lointein,

        Leur harmonie et ordre irrevocable
        Se tourneroit en erreur variable,
        Et comme moy travailleroient en vain.

21) What figure, height and shade of hair are fittest
      To make a man admired? and what complexion?
      What colour of eye most sweetens the affection?
      Which deals the heart a deadly wound the quickest?

      For a man's voice, which song has truest feeling?
      And of the saddest songs which pierces deeper?
      Which causes the sweet lute to ring still sweeter?
      Which type of character's the most appealing?

      I would not like to speak my mind for sure
      For Love has prejudiced my heart and eyes,
      But I will guess, and think I am no liar,

      That all the beauty we most keenly prize
      And all the art that may improve on Nature
      Could not increase the strength of my desire.

22) Glittering Sun, how happily you gaze
      For ever on your mistress' face! and you,
      His sister, in Endymion's embrace,
      Drink to repletion of love's honeydew!

      Mars looks on Venus; Mercury the bold
      Ventures from Sky to Sky; revisiting
      The places of his hot and bawdy spring,
      Jupiter's reconciled with growing old.

      Such is the potent harmony of Heaven,
      The bond that each to each links the divine;
      But if their present loves were distant ever,

      That indissoluble serenity
      Would into error drift and vagary,
      And all their labour be as vain as mine.

23) Las! que me sert, que si parfaitement
      Louas jadis et ma tresse doree,
      Et de mes yeus la beauté comparee
      A deus Soleils, dont Amour finement

      Tira les trets causes de ton tourment?
      Ou estes vous, pleurs de peu de duree?
      Et Mort par qui devoit estre honoree
      Ta ferme amour et iteré serment?

      Donques c'estoit le but de ta malice
      De m'asservir sous ombre de service?
      Pardonne moy, Ami, à cette fois,

      Estant outree et de despit et d'ire:
      Mais je m'assure, quelque part que tu sois,
      Qu'autant que moy tu soufres de martire.

24) Ne reprenez, Dames, si j'ay aymé:
      Si j'ay senti mile torches ardentes,
      Mile travaus, mile douleurs mordentes:
      Si en pleurant, j'ay mon tems consumé,

      Las que mon nom n'en soit par vous blamé.
      Si j'ay failli, les peines sont presentes,
      N'aigrissez point leurs pointes violentes:
      Mais estimez qu'Amour, à point nommé,

      Sans votre ardeur d'un Vulcan excuser,
      Sans la beauté d'Adonis acuser,
      Pourra, s'il veut, plus vous rendre amoureuses:

      En ayant moins que moy d'ocasion,
      Et plus d'estrange et forte passion.
      Et gardez vous d'estre plus malheureuses.

3) What good is it to me that once you praised
     The silk perfection of my golden hair,
     Or that to two bright Suns you would compare
     The beauty of my eyes, from which Love gazed

     And shot the burning darts so expertly?
     Where are you now, tears that so quickly dried?
     Or death, which was to prove you would abide
     By oath of love and solemn fealty?

     Or did you seek from malice to delude,
     Enslaving by pretending servitude?
     Forgive the thought, my dearest love, this once

     When grief and anger piercingly combine:
     I tell myself, wherever you may chance
     To be, your martyrdom's as harsh as mine.

4) Do not reproach me, ladies, if I've loved
     And felt a thousand torches burn my veins,
     A thousand griefs, a thousand biting pains.
     If all my days to bitter tears dissolved,

     Then, ladies, do not denigrate my name.
     If I did wrong, the pain and punishment
     Are now. Don't file their needles to a point.
     Consider: Love is master of the game:

     No need of Vulcan to explain your fire,
     Nor of Adonis to excuse desire,
     But with less cause than mine, far less occasion,

     As the whim takes him, idly he can curse
     You with a stranger and a stronger passion.
     But O take care your suffering's not worse.

SONNET 1

Many editors simply omit this Italian sonnet which Louise Labé placed at the head of her collection of poems. She did, however, intend it to be part of them and so it must be included. It is something of an embarrassment, since it is clearly an academic exercise, giving quite a different picture of the author from the usual one of someone who is totally spontaneous and sensual. We must not forget that the whole sequence is artificial, however closely it may seem to be related to real experience, and that even the triteness of the language of love may re-present in a very real way the experience. The conventional way of expressing the experience ultimately becomes an important part of the experience. It is only in this way that we can reconcile the uniqueness and yet at the same time the ordinariness of any love-experience.

I do not wish to say much more about this sonnet, because any meaningful assessment of it would have to consider its relation to the whole tradition and this would take us too far afield. B. L. Nicholas writes of it 'The opening sonnet of the series is portentously bad' (because it 'shamelessly strings together the most hackneyed commonplaces of Petrarchism').[1] I am inclined to agree with this judgement but I would not put the case quite as strongly as that. I see the poem rather as a light introduction, not intended to be taken so seriously, and a conscious link with the Petrarchan tradition from which she is going to depart, and as serving to introduce several of the elements which will be important throughout the sequence (e.g., 'i begli ochi'). In l.12 Giudici wants to amend the text to 'Chieggioti' to make Louise continue to refer to Love and not to Fate as the grammar requires, because the original reading makes the sonnet less efficacious, less dramatic, and more involved.[2] (I have given the original text, but it has been translated according to the best sense.)

SONNET 2

In a sense this sonnet is the first in the sequence, since the Italian sonnet, because of its language, is necessarily different from the rest, and has a greater degree of artificiality.

Many of the sonnets in this sequence begin rather tritely, and then continue in a more original manner; so the Italian sonnet and this first French sonnet form a trite beginning to the whole sequence. They give the traditional starting-point, the pattern from which she will diverge. The first words (already used in Italian) are a sort of poetic counter or token, current coin at the time in the language of poets. This, in fact, is often the way in which she practises imitation: she quotes, not so much from particular poets as from the common stock.

The traditional series of antitheses, emphasized by the use of apostrophe, is also important, because the following sonnets will refer back to them, by repetition and variation. The repeated use of these commonplace words of the language of love and of the language of the poetry of love, together with the subtly varied combinations in which they appear, expresses the ordinariness and yet privileged particularity of the experience of love.

The sequence begins with this invocation to the eyes as does the *Délie* of Maurice Scève ('L'Œil trop ardent en mes jeunes erreurs'), since in the Platonist-Petrarchan philosophy of love, love first enters into a person through the senses and the eyes were the first of the senses to apprehend the beloved. The colour of the eyes is not important since the phrase is a commonplace, cf. Ronsard, *Amours*, s.25, l.1. 'Ces deux yeulx bruns, deux flambeaulx de ma vie'. In l.1 the change from 'yeus' to 'regars' makes for greater intimacy; 'regars' is more personal, more active than 'yeus'. We find in ll.1–2 a confusion of persons which will continue throughout the sequence. The 'beaus yeus bruns' are certainly those of her lover; the 'regars', at this stage, could be either his or hers, and l.2 could refer to either. Certainly by the time we reach l.3 it is her own experience she is thinking of. 'Destournez' shows that the loved one will not return her loving gaze.

The third and fourth lines show her helplessness in the face of external forces, the inevitability of the natural alternation of day and night which brings home to her the continued absence of the loved one, and her frustration. In the opening line the author had started to evoke his physical presence; she will continue this in the first tercet 'Ô ris, ô front. . . .', with pathetic longing. In between there are seven lines of bitter melancholic regret and self-pity. This is achieved especially by the falling rhythm at the ends of ll.2–3, and the insistent 'du' sound ('espandues', 'atendues' later picked up again in 'perdus', 'despendues' and 'tendues') which expresses a past tense, but one which carries over into the present so that both times are communicated simultaneously, cf. *Élégie* I, ll.35–6.

> En voyant tant de larmes espandues,
> Tant de souspirs et prieres perdues.
> [Seeing so many tears shed, so many sighs and un-requited prayers.]

At the end of l.4 'retournez' raises us up to the original level, and turns the whole quatrain back on itself, including and embracing it. ('Retournez' contains '*re*gars des*tournez*' just as 'destinez' (l.8) contains the '*de*sirs ob*stinez*' of l.5.)

To counteract the incoherent accumulation of ll.1–8 (not, of course, that incoherence is a defect in love-poetry, nor, indeed, accumulation) there is in l.9, a definite progression from the whole face right down to the finger tips.

In l.10 'viole' is perhaps quite unambiguous, though the violence of emotion is to play an important part in the whole sequence (see, for example, *24*.7, 'N'aigrissez point leurs pointes violentes'). In this same line 10 there is a stress on the vocal element in love, the attractiveness and musicality of the voice, the voice of a poet and musician with its incantatory charm (carmen), cf. *Élégie* III, ll.3–4:

> Quand mes regrets, ennuis, despits et larmes
> M'orrez chanter en pitoyables carmes,
> [When you hear me relate in pitiful songs my sufferings, griefs, afflictions and tears.]

There is in *Le débat* a discussion of the relation between music and love, and singing and harmony are called the effect and sign of perfect love.

In this connection I wish to draw attention to the multiple internal rhymes and cross-references within this sonnet, which will appear also in all the other sonnets, both individually and as a sequence. Since it will be impossible for me to point them all out, the present sonnet will serve as a model for the way in which I think they should all be read. 'Beaus' rhymes internally with 'chaus', 'maus' and 'flambeaus', and 'yeus' with 'cheveus', 'feus' and 'iceus'. Sometimes the internal rhyme is linked with the end-rhymes, for example, 'noires', 'doits', 'toy', 'endrois'. Sometimes words are clearly linked by sound though not themselves identical in sound: 'soupirs', 'noires nuits', 'tristes', 'desirs', 'rets', 'pires', 'ris', and sometimes it is the ideas rather than the sounds, which are linked: 'chaus', 'flambeaus', 'feus', 'estincelle': in the same way, in l.9, 'front' sums up all of the first line. In l.9 'mains' reminds us of 'pleins' (l.5) which is immediately echoed in 'Ô lut pleintif' and 'de toy me plein'. This particular sound is one which is in very great evidence throughout the sequence, as is the sound, expressing futility and the passage of time contained in 'nuits' and 'luisans'.

The last tercet needs some elucidation. It seems clear that 'toy' refers to the man, though it is difficult at first reading not to link it with 'lut'; (since, of course, 'lut' could also stand for the man here, the confusion is even more obvious). The syntax suggests a further ambiguity. Louise Labé often leaves us in some doubt about the true subject of a verb, particularly of a present participle. At first we are not absolutely sure whether 'portant' refers to the man or to herself. In the end we conclude that it refers to 'toy', because it is the man who carries 'tant de flambeaus'; in the same way, in l.13, 'toy' is the subject of 'tatant' and 'mon cœur' is the object. 'D'iceus' would then mean 'with them', i.e., 'feus'. After that there is a new subject 'estincelle'. This distorted syntax, and especially the holding over of the verbs until the end of the lines, produces a slowing-up effect.

To the reader of the time the word 'estincelle' would have been a significant one, for two reasons; firstly, because the spark which was at the origin of the experience of love was part of the Petrarchan tradition (cf. Ronsard, *Amours*, s.136, ll.1–4: 'De ton poil d'or en tresses blondissant,/Amour ourdit de son arc la ficelle,/Il me tira de ta vive estincelle,/Le doulx fier traict, qui me tient languissant' [From your gold-tressed hair, Love wove his bow-string; from your living spark he shot at me the sweet and cruel shaft which keeps me languishing.]), and secondly, because it was used frequently in the writings of the Neo-platonists for the first stirrings of the divine influence within our souls, whether in the experience of love, of writing poetry or just of knowledge in general.

It is to be noted that the quatrains appear also, word for word, in sonnet 55 of the *Souspirs* of Olivier de Magny, not published until 1557, which is why most critics are agreed that the sonnet refers to him. It is not, however, clear what the exact relation between the sonnets is.

I have dwelt at some length on this sonnet which some critics reject out of hand as a mere exercise in verse-writing, because it seems to me that it is intentionally a traditional sonnet (the technique, for example, of beginning almost every line with 'Ô' is found frequently in the love-poetry of the time cf., especially, Ronsard, *Amours*, s.173: 'Ô traits fichez dans le but de mon ame') in which Louise Labé wishes to show that she does not despise the common language of love and love-poetry, and because, in spite of all that it owes to the tradition, we can at least sense the depth of her own feeling.

SONNET 3

The first three words sum up the frustration of the previous sonnet, and stress the apparent eternity of its duration. 'Esperances vaines' is a common expression in this tradition of love-poetry; it gains some originality here by the echo of 'vainement atendues' of the earlier sonnet. In the transference of 'longs desirs' and 'tristes soupirs' from 'chaus soupirs', 'tristes pleins' and 'desirs obstinez' we see, in the way in which the poet transposes her epithets, the slight and almost imperceptible variations she feels in the experience of love. By now the tears are 'coutumieres', doubly so, to her and to us, and there is a certain self-consciousness, both in her universalizing statement and in our reaction to the situation. (Without being as wary, of course of the cliché as is the modern writer, Louise is conscious of it fully. The sonnets progress from a conventional setting in the first eight lines to an intense and individual one in the sestet, and perhaps this is why one feels her to be so real a poet—the wrapping is skilfully removed from the emotion).* 'Coutumieres/A' is typical of the strong use of prepositions in Louise Labé, and indeed in the sixteenth century in general; the preposition after 'coutumiere' is always 'de', as in modern French, and as it is in Louise Labé's second *Élégie*, ll.33–4. Although there is nothing new in the fountain imagery of ll.3–4, we are instantly reminded of his eyes ('O beaus yeus bruns'), almost to the point of confusing the two. 'Regars' (l.6) refers us back to the 'regars destournez'; the cruelty of the loved one is contrasted with the sympathy shown by the stars. The contrast gains by the fact that the stars would normally be supposed to be largely responsible for her fate. Line 5 speaks both of the inhumanity of the man who can let her suffer in this way, and of the wretchedness of man's condition; 'inhumaines' and 'celestes' are contrasted, though they have an area where their meanings overlap. 'Transi' seems to have been usually a much stronger word at the time than it is today, meaning either literally 'dead' or 'transported outside oneself'. (Cotgrave has: '*transi*. Fallen into a traunce, or sowne; whose heart, sense, or vitall spirits faile him; astonied, amazed, appalled, halfe-dead'). Here it is linked with 'cœur', but refers directly to herself. It is one of several violent adjectives, originally past participles, used by the author, cf., also 'navree' in l.12 below. Luc van Brabant sees 'cœur transi' as a leitmotif of the poetry of Olivier de Magny, relates it to Louise Labé's device 'Je meurs de jour et brusle la nuyct' by his technique of anagrams, and says it always refers to her when he uses it (cf. *Odes amoureuses* (1559), no. xiv, 'D'une devise que luy donna s'Amye dans un anneau. Je meurs de jour, et brusle denuyct. Ode'. The same motto is to be found in Emblem xlv accompanying the *Délie* of Maurice Scève (*Le iour meurs et la nuict ars*), and in the following dizain (402). It is, in fact, a common expression in the poets). 'Croitre' should be taken transitively (=accroître, augmenter, see Huguet's dictionary), because she wishes to stress her own diminished responsibility, in the face of some outside force which leads her on to love (cf. 2.8, 'Ô pires maus contre moi destinez' with its determination and inevitability). Cotgrave, on the other hand, shows *croistre* as intransitive, and *accroistre* as both transitive and intransitive.

In l.10 'nouveaus feus' refers back to the long list ('tant de feus') of sonnet 2, and 'en toutes pars' refers back to 'En tant d'endrois' (2.13). 'Se despiter' is another of the verbs expressing emotion which have a weaker meaning in modern French than they had in the sixteenth century. Cotgrave gives: 'To be exceeding angrie; to fret, fume, chafe, stomacke extreamley; to take in great scorne, dudgeon, or snuffe'.

There is a clear link in this sonnet between l.8 and ll.13–14. Line 8 had suggested that it would be impossible for her to suffer more, and the last two lines of the poem make the point more explicit. The 'nouvelle plaie' is contrasted with the 'larmes coutumieres' of the first quatrain. 'Empirer', according to Huguet, had three meanings in the sixteenth century,

'altérer, nuire à (blesser), outrager': it is the second meaning
which is most suitable here. In the context the word contains
also something of the 'pires maus' of 2.8. For *navré*, Cotgrave
has: 'Wounded, hurt; afflicted vexed; nipped sorely, wrung
extreamely.'

The ending of the sonnet shows clarity and incisiveness, intensity and determination, as so often in this sequence.

SONNET 4

This sonnet describes the vicissitudes and the conflict of love.

In the first quatrain the close link between the image of
poison and that of fire is well brought out; love is the poison
which eats up (consumes) the innermost being of its victim.
There is a clear connection between 'empoisonna' and 'fureur',
since 'fureur' was often associated and even equated with
'frenesie' a physical as well as psychological disturbance. In
the *Nouvelle continuation des amours* (1556) Ronsard clearly
links love and illness, cf. Chanson, 'Je ne veulx plus que
chanter de tristesse', ll.73–80:

> Amour vrayement est une maladie,/Les medecins la
> scavent bien juger,/L'appellant mal, fureur de fantasie/
> Qui ne se peult par herbes soulager./J'aymerois mieux la
> fiebvre dans mes venes,/Ou quelque peste, ou quelqu'autre
> douleur,/Que de souffrir tant d'amoureuses peines,/Qui
> sans tüer me consomment le cueur.' [Love truly is a
> malady: doctors judge it well when they call it sickness,
> fantastic madness which can't be cured by herbs. I would
> rather have a fever in my veins, or some plague or other
> affliction, than suffer so many pains of love, which consume
> my heart without killing me.]

In *Élégie* I Louise writes: 'Qui [sc. le mal] me persa d'une
telle furie,/Qu'encor n'en suis apres long tems guerie:' [Which
(i.e. the sickness) shot me through with such frenzy that I am
still not cured of it a long time afterwards.] (ll.39–40). In an
article on 'Louise Labé and Marsilio Ficino' in *Modern Language Notes*,[3] Professor Varty shows that she took from
Ficino 'the theory of love passing between the eyes of people
as a vapour and infecting them like a germ, resulting in a sickness which is love'.

The juxtaposition of 'Amour' and 'cruel' shows that Louise

Labé wishes to shift responsibility even further away from herself than she did in the previous sonnet; here she makes it clear that the loved one himself is not entirely to blame: it is not only he who is 'cruel' but the god Love, 'Cil qui les Dieus et les hommes mesprise'. The lover is not to blame for his cruelty to her, because the god is no respecter of persons and is responsible for the whole situation. We shall see later in the sequence how Louise makes excuses for the man.

'Premierement' reminds us of the 'passions premieres' of 3.7; the present sonnet picks up again a theme which will become increasingly more evident, that of duration (her long wait for her lover, and the different stages of the experience); this is not the same as the theme, more usual in the love-poetry of the period, of the passage of time and the urgent need to make the most of the present. In this sonnet the theme is conveyed particularly in the words 'Depuis qu' . . . Premierement . . . Tousjours . . . un seul jour . . . tousjours', and in spite of the use of the tense 'brulay' we must understand a perfect tense, something which carries through until the time of writing. When I have said that these temporal words tell us something about the stages of the experience I do not mean to suggest that there is a very clear chronological structure to the poems with a counterpart in the reality of the experience. Most critics would agree that this is not the case, or, at least, that because of the lack of evidence we do not know whether it is the case or not, though Luc van Brabant feels that it is quite possible to ascribe with certainty particular sonnets to particular lovers, and even to particular dates.

'Fureur divine' reminds us that it is the *god* of Love Louise is talking about (and this in turn recalls the 'celestes lumieres' of 3.6), and tells us that love is to be taken in the Neo-platonic context of the four furies. I do not think that she wished to insist on this point, nor that she felt that the experience of love was anything other than purely human. Nevertheless, since she consciously uses the terminology and mythology current at the time, then her love-poetry must be understood in this context. Certainly her contemporaries were well aware of the way she was using the ideas then in vogue.

The idea of divine fury was an essential part of the system of Neo-platonic thought. In so far as France was concerned, by the time Louise Labé wrote, the idea of divine fury as the origin of all the arts and as the basis of love had been completely assimilated, largely through the editions and translations of Ficino, and of Plato.

It is worth comparing the present sonnet with the beginning of the first *Élégie*, in which a distinction is made between the fury of love and that which drives her to write love-poetry.

> Au tems qu'Amour, d'hommes et Dieus vainqueur,
> Faisoit bruler de sa flamme mon cœur
> En embrassant de sa cruelle rage
> Mon sang, mes os, mon esprit et courage.
>
> [When Love, conqueror of men and Gods made my heart burn with his flame, with his cruel fury taking possession of my blood, my bones, my mind and heart.]

At this stage, she writes, Phœbus did not allow her to compose poetry,

> Mais maintenant que sa fureur divine
> Remplit d'ardeur ma hardie poitrine,
> Chanter me fait . . . (ll.9–11)
>
> [But now that his divine frenzy fills my dauntless heart with ardour, he makes me sing.]

There is in ll.4–5 of the sonnet a strong break between 'abandonna' and 'Quelque' which brings out the absoluteness and insistent quality of her pain. 'Travail' means both labour, trouble and torment; Cotgrave gives: 'Travell, toile, teene, labour, businesse, pains-taking; trouble, molestation, care'. It is to be contrasted with 'repos': cf. *Élégie* III, ll.66–7.

In the second quatrain it is possible that 'menasse' is merely the threat of coming torment, which would be of concern only to herself, but 'procheine ruïne' is very much more, and has a direct social (if not ethical) relevance. The words are significant if we wish to understand the comments she makes elsewhere to the 'dames lyonnaises'. The threat is, of course, a real one; it is threefold, the threat of discovery by her husband, of the lover's desertion of her, and of public disgrace. This adds the same intensity to the poetry as it does to the experience. The inversion 'procheine ruïne' slows up the line emphatically. 'Ruïne' calls forth the idea of death in the next line; death is used here both literally and metaphorically. These two lines are illustrations of the author's delight in absolutes ('qui tout termine,/De rien. . . .')

As is often the case with verbs of emotion in the sixteenth

century 's'estonna' is much stronger and more violent than today. Huguet gives as equivalents 's'ébranler, s'endommager, s'effrayer', and if we look at Estienne's *Dictionnaire francois latin* (1549) we find 'Conturbare, Horrificare, Obtundere, Stupefacere'; Cotgrave has for *estonner*: 'To astonish, amaze, daunt, appall; abash, put out of countenance; make agast; also, to stonnie, benumme, or dull the sences of'.

In the tercets the construction 'Tant plus qu'. . . .' expresses again absoluteness and intensity and contains, too, the idea of duration. We are reminded of 'Depuis qu'Amour' (l.1) and 'Qu'encor Amour' (*3.9*).

'Nous' (l.9) is generic; this is a proverbial account of love which includes the reader in the statement, but it is applicable particularly to herself and the lover, though the lover is here, at least apparently, not touched by love.

The tercets tell of the supremacy and arbitrariness of love in all amorous encounters. The military metaphors were commonplace, cf., for example, Ronsard, *Le premier livre des amours*, s.*1*, ll.1–2 'Qui voudra voyr comme un Dieu me surmonte,/Comme il m'assault, comme il se fait vainqueur . . .' and Louise, herself, in the *Élégies* uses many military metaphors, for example, I, ll.25–7,

> Il m'est avis que je sen les alarmes,
>
> Que premiers j'u d'Amour, je voy les armes,
>
> Dont il s'arma en venant m'assaillir.
>
> [I know I feel the first alarums I had of Love, I see his weapons with which he armed himself on coming to assail me.]

See also *Élégie* III, ll.49–53:

> j'ai subjugué les Dieus
>
> En bas Enfers, en la mer et es Cieus.
>
> Et penses tu que n'aye tel pouvoir
>
> Sur les humeins, de leur faire savoir
>
> Qu'il n'y a rien qui de ma main eschape?
>
> [I have subdued the Gods of the Underworld, of the sea and the Heavens. And do you think that I have not the same power over human beings, to make them realize that there is nothing that escapes my influence?]

Commentaries

SONNET 5

This sonnet introduces us to the deeply passionate poetry
usually associated with Louise Labé. The appeal to Venus is
partly a prayer ('Entens ma voix . . .') to the goddess of love
(from whom she seems to expect greater sympathy than from
the god of Love), and partly, and more directly, a reference
to the planet Venus, which puts her own experience on to a
more cosmic level. Many of the poets of the time discussed
the theme that it is by love that one takes part in the cosmic
processes of nature. See, for example, Ronsard, in the *Hymne
de la mort*

> Et ne fut de Venus l'ame generative,
> Qui tes fautes repare, et rend la forme vive,
> Le monde perirait; mais son germe en refait
> Autant de son coté que ton dard en defait[4]
> [And were it not for the life-giving power of Venus,
> which repairs your faults and gives back the living form,
> the world would perish; but her seed remakes as many as
> your arrow destroys.]

Luc van Brabant makes great play of the fact that Venus was
the star under which Louise was born.[5] Apart altogether from
the doubt about the date of her birth, most of his proof seems
to come from a poem by Guillaume Aubert, published in
her honour, which speaks of 'Venus, sa douce mere'. This
does appear too general to be conclusive, though it is quite
possible that she saw herself as under the special protection of
Venus.

The wandering of Venus ('erres par les Cieus') recalls the
arbitrariness of love in the preceding sonnet. Calepin's
Dictionary (edition of 1553-4) has: 'Est item Venus, una
errantium stellarum, inter Solis et Mercurii sphaeras sita, quae
φωσφόρος Graecè, Lucifer Latinè dicitur, quum antegreditur
Solem: quum autem subsequitur, Hesperos, Vesper, et Ves-
perugo.' [Venus is one of the wandering stars, situated between
the spheres of the Sun and Mercury, and is called the Light-
Bringer in Greek and Latin when it precedes the Sun; when
however it follows the Sun, it is called the Evening Star.]
(We might also compare the beginning of Scève's *Délie*,
quoted above,

> L'Œil trop ardent en mes jeunes erreurs
> Girouettait mal cault, a l'impourveue:

[My eyes, too ardent in my first wanderings, turned like a weather-cock, imprudent and idle.])

In l.2 'ma voix' is her own personal voice, and at the same time the voice of her poetry. 'Chantera' causes some slight difficulty; she will continue to address her prayer to Venus as long as Venus shines in the sky: this could mean either (i) during the night, but only then, or, (ii) every night, for ever. The rest of the poem shows that the first meaning is the principal one. There is a parallel in the first *Élégie* (ll.14–17):

Il [sc. Phebus] m'a donné la lyre, qui les vers
Souloit chanter de l'Amour Lesbienne:
Et à ce coup pleurera de la mienne.
O dous archet, adouci moy la vois . . .

[He (sc. Phœbus) gave me the lyre, which used to sing poems of Sapphic love, and will now make lament for mine. O sweet bow, sweeten my voice.]

'Ta face' recalls 'front' of *2.9*, and 'Piteus regars des celestes lumieres' (*3.6*); (cf., also, l.8 'voyant témoins tes yeus'). There is a contrast made between 'Ta face' and 'mon œil'. By making Venus personal in this way, the poet brings out closely the relation between man and the universe. (Why, we may ask, will her 'œil veillant s'atendrir bien mieux'? Because Venus is a visible reminder 1) of her pain 2) of the power of love 3) of the universality of her situation.)*

'Travail' (l.4), with the meaning of 'sorrow' or 'worry', refers back immediately to 'Quelque travail' (*4.5*) which appears in the same place in the line, though not in the same line in the sonnet. 'Souci' forms a direct link with 'menasse et procheine ruïne' (*4.6*) understood in the threefold sense suggested above. 'Ennuieus' has a multiplicity of meanings at the time, all of them much stronger than the modern French sense of 'boring'. The Estienne dictionary gives the following: 'Acerbus, Odiosus, Incommodus' and Cotgrave: 'Troublesome, displeasing, offensive; grievous; loathsome, wearisome, tedious, irksome; distastfull; most importunate.' When Du Bellay talks in *Les regrets* of his 'ennuis' he is not speaking of minor irritations but of a profound melancholy resulting from serious personal misfortunes.

'Veillant' recalls the long vigils of *2.3–4*, 'Ô noires nuits'. Luc van Brabant sees this sonnet as an illustration of her motto, 'je meurs de jour et brusle la nuyct'.

The second quatrain illustrates two techniques often used by the author, the use of the present participle to stress continuous duration, and the use of comparatives to produce greater intensity.

From the point of view of the structure of the poem there is a parallel between 'Ciel/Cieus', 'œil/Yeus' and 'travail/travaus'.

The tercets contain the first truly sensual description we have yet seen in the poems, but this effect is not achieved by means of what is described so much as by the form of the poem, its structure and its sounds. 'Donq' appears to introduce a logical element into the poem, but it should be read either as a vague temporal link or even as disrupting logical sequence. It is often used to translate not the Latin 'ergo' or 'igitur' but 'nempe' with its great spread of meanings, serving merely to indicate transition from one point or subject to another. 'Humains' is used (recalling 'inhumaines' of *3.5*) because she is still addressing herself to Venus. Lines 9–10 are successful because of the 's' sounds and the involved inversions. The whole couplet starts with an inversion, then comes a minor one in 'les lassez esprits', and another major one in 'De dous repos'. The total effect is a stress on the word 'lassez'. The inversion 'lassez esprits' is good largely because this poem has so many verbs at the end of the line, which are weak rhymes but strong verbs. Lines 9–10 are isolated from the rest of the poem to show that Louise does not share this happy release which the rest of mankind is able to find in sleep. She is 'esprise' with something much more violent. (For *espris* Cotgrave has: 'Taken, surprised, seised; also, inflamed, kindled, wholly possessed with'). There is a definite hiatus between lines 10 and 11. 'J'endure mal' is a further summary of much that has gone before: 'endure' contains the 'durtez' of *3.5* and also the painfulness of duration; 'luit' contains the 'jours luisans' (*2.4*) and 'luira' (*5.3*); 'soleil' is a partial internal rhyme with 'sommeil'.

The last tercet is one of the most memorable in the whole collection. Its success is due to the violence and, at the same time, sensual calm of its sounds:

Et quand je *suis* qua*si* [toute] ça*ss*ee,

Et que *m*e *suis* *m*i*s*e en *m*on *l*it *la*ssee,

Crier *m*e faut *m*on *mal* [toute] la n*ui*t.

The crossing of the sounds here is particularly effective, the hard 'c' sound alternating with, and then in the last line giving place to, the softer 'm' and 'l'. There are also many references back to the rest of the poem (to the rest of the experience which the poem is). When, for example, we read 'mise en mon lit lassee' we automatically read into this the 'mol' of 'mon lit mol' (l.7), and the 'nuit' of the last line reminds us of the other time it was used (2.3). Here perhaps it is relevant to remember the poem of Sappho which most nearly approaches those of Louise Labé:

Δέδυκε μὲν ἀ σελάνα,
Καὶ Πληϊαδες, μέσαι δὲ
Νύκτες, παρὰ δ'ἔρχεθ'ὥρα
'Εγὼ δὲ μόνα καθεύδω,

[The moon has set, and the Pleiades, midnight is gone, the hour is past, and I lie alone.]

already published in 1554 by Henri Estienne in his edition of Anacreon.[6]

It is interesting to note that it was translated by Ronsard in the second book of *Amours*:

Desia la Lune est couchée,
La poussinière est cachée,
Et ia la my-nuict brunette
Vers l'Aurore s'est panchée,
Et ie dors au lict seulette.

[The moon has set already, the Pleiades are hidden, already dark midnight has inclined towards dawn, and I sleep in bed alone.]

'Quasi toute cassee' is not used merely for the sound; the first word attenuates, but only slightly, the absoluteness of 'toute'; the poet knows she is not utterly broken, and is capable of even further suffering. This last tercet is a further explanation of 's'atendrira' (l.5); her 'tendresse' is her inability ('crier me *faut*') to dominate her emotions.

(It is the simplicity and directness of the last three lines which somehow convey a real human voice.)*

SONNET 6

This sonnet possesses an obscurity which is rare in Louise Labé. Most commentators have managed to interpret it or translate it without any apparent difficulty but unfortunately they have arrived at very different interpretations about what it actually means. There is the initial problem of what 'ce cler Astre' refers to. Cotgrave gives: '*Astre*, a Starre, a Planet; also destinie, fate, fortune, hap. *Astre argenté*, The Moone; *Astre cornu*, The same; *L'Astre du jour*, The Sunne.' It might seem obvious at first reading that it means the sun, but certain critics argue with some plausibility that it is Venus (*Clere Venus*, the day-star). We may compare Henri Estienne's note in the *Dialogue du langage français italianisé* (quoted in Huguet): 'Quant au soleil et à la lune, leurs noms leur demeurent. Mais quant aux estoiles, le courtisan les appelle plus volontiers astres qu'estoiles, usans du mot poetique'. [As for Sun and Moon, they keep their names. But as for the stars, the courtier more readily calls them luminaries than stars, using the poetic word.] Whichever it is, 'Astre' seems also to stand for her lover (whether it be Olivier de Magny here as Dorothy O'Connor suggested, or Henri II according to Luc van Brabant)[7] whom she wants to come to release her from the 'travail' of the night. We have already seen that the mere coming of the day is not sufficient ('Ô jours luisans vainement retournez'). The present sonnet is a poem of renewal, an optimistic counterpart to s.2.

The first line has a Virgilian ring about it; the expression was a fairly common one in sixteenth-century French poetry.

We notice again the references to sight and the eye: 'cler', 'œil' and 'regarder'.

The second main area of disagreement about what this poem means comes in the interpretation of 'Ce que . . . Que celle . . . Qu'elle . . . Qui . . .'. Three of the English translations, for example, give, for the first 'ce que': 'whatever' (Alta Lind Cook), 'the one on whom' (Lobb), and 'they on whom' (Prokosch). Van Brabant has 'al wie' (all whom) and Giudici 'Ciò ch' ('whatever'). It seems to me that there is no sufficient reason to take 'ce que' in any other than its normal sense of 'whatever'; no need to take it as though 'ce que' referred to herself; and, in fact, such a view merely complicates the poem without giving it richer resonances.

It is important to see clearly what is the syntactical structure of the next few lines. Lines 4–5 are parallel to one another and express an exclamation, 'How she will . . .' 'Celle là' looks forward to the 'qui' of l.6, which stands for 'celle qui'. 'Un bon tour' refers to her good fortune; Huguet gives for it 'bienfait, service, bon procédé.'

'Le plus beau don de Flore' has been variously interpreted. For Giudici it is the rose 'to which Louise compares the lips of the loved one',[8] (though Louise could easily, if she had wished, have used rose-imagery in her poetry, except perhaps that it traditionally referred to the woman). For Van Brabant it is Spring, or eternal youth, which is symbolically a flower. (He points out that Spring is the child of Flora and Zephyrus, and then explains 'le mieus sentant que jamais vid Aurore' as 'Youth, the most beautiful god, fragrant as Spring, with whom the amorous Love could always fall in love'.) He feels that Louise is asking Venus, the goddess of beauty, to let her always remain young and fresh.

In the tercets, 'C'est à moy seule' makes clear the general idea of the quatrains, and emphasizes her own loneliness which we have already seen; here the placing together of 'moy' and 'seule', although this is not the primary meaning of the phrase, is surely intentional. (Note the engaging unselfconscious delight in and anticipation of her own luck—again, this is the poet's authentic voice.)* The next line is a good summary and reminder of the preceding sonnets; we, the readers, have already been present during much of the 'tant de pleurs et tant de tems perdu', since the reference is as much to the lamentations which go to make up her poetry as to her sleepless nights. The particular reference is to *2.2*, *3.2* and *5.6*. The falling rhythm and the 'du' sound at the end of the line have already been commented on in the notes to s.2. The phrase 'O tems perdu' has been used once before (*2.6*) but at the beginning of the line. In the same way 'le voyant' (l.10) echoes 'te voyant' (*5.6*) but comes in a different place in the line. These self-quotations are not mere trite and incompetent repetitions, but provide a slight and subtle variation of mood, and help to link together, by the power of memory, the various stages or moments of the experience.

Huguet says of 'faire feste de qqn.': 'en faire l'éloge, le vanter, en parler beaucoup', and Cotgrave has '*Faire feste à*. To flatter, smooth, faune on, make fayre weather unto'; and '*Faire feste de*. To joy in, rejoyce at, be glad of; to brag, boast, be proud, make much of'.

I do not think that we need pay too much attention to the

military metaphor in the last tercet, and conclude that this proves that the sonnet was written for the 'homme de guerre'. Such metaphors were a commonplace of the writing of love-poetry, even with reference to the woman (think of Petrarch's 'dolce nemica' and Chaucer's 'swete fo' and the many other military images which appear in the present sequence). For example, here, apart from 'feray grande conqueste' we have 'de mes yeus le pouvoir', and cf., also, 'combats' (*4.*11), and 'Tant plus qu'Amour nous vient fort assaillir' (*4.9*). This poem is, of course, more optimistic than the previous one; this is conveyed in part by the striking 'peu de temps' which contrasts sharply with 'toute la nuit', and also with the 'tems perdu' of s.2 and l.10 of the present poem.

SONNET 7

The first two lines, and especially the first, are a good example of the way in which Louise Labé likes to progress from a trite, even proverbial expression to something which is more original, more direct and urgent. The impersonal, universal truth is then followed by the application of it to herself, once again, inserting her own experience into the cosmic order. The absoluteness ('toute chose animee') recalls 'mort qui tout termine' of *4.7*. There is an abruptness in ll.3–4, an impatience with the general statement of ll.1–2, which makes for the very fast movement of ll.3–4.

The immediate meaning of l.3 is: 'When you go away or are absent, you leave me dead; when you are with me you give me life as the soul gives the body life'. The author, however, is saying much more than this. She sees herself as the body, delights in and wishes to 'recognize' her sensuality. She does not expect that the man would be able to say the same thing to her.

This first quatrain makes use of varied sentence structure, a general statement followed by a temporal clause, a particular statement which explains the first one, followed by a question. Then in l.5 we have an imperative. The effect of this variety is to show the rapidly changing mood of the poet. The simple question in l.4 expresses tenderness and great longing. If we think back over the sonnets we have read so far we see that we do not in fact know where the lover is.

'Pasmee' is another of those words expressing a present emotional state by means of a past participle; the word some-times has a stronger emotional charge than its modern counter-part (cf. Des Autels, *Repos*, quoted in Huguet, 'Est ce point une ecstase qui me pasme / Et me ravit en contemplation ?').

There is a textual difficulty in l.5. It seems that the author wrote the plural 'laissez' which is odd after the singular 'tu' throughout. Perhaps it is just a mistake which was not correc-ted even in the second edition. Giudici suggests that the text is correct, but that Louise would have pronounced it 'laisse' according to sixteenth-century usage.

The second quatrain is rich and full and is greatly enhanced by the ambiguity of 'ton corps' which can be taken literally referring to him as well as continuing the initial allegory. The reason for 'viendrois trop tard' is not quite clear, or rather it has a twofold meaning. There is the suggestion that if he does not return then she will really die, and there may also be the hint that she will no longer need him; cf. *Élégie* II, ll.93–8:

> Revien donq tot, si tu as quelque envie
> De me revoir encor un coup en vie.
> Et si la mort avant ton arrivee
> Ha de mon corps l'aymante ame privee,
> Au moins un jour vien, habillé de dueil,
> Environner le tour de mon cercueil.
> [Come back soon, if you have any wish to see me still alive. And if death has deprived my body of its loving soul before your arrival, still come some day, dressed in mourning, to walk around my coffin.]

These quatrains (especially because of 'meilleure part' and 'moitié estimée') are often supposed to have Neo-platonic overtones. If they have I am not sure that this amounts to very much. The most we can say is that there is possibly a slight reference to the myth of the Androgyne, and to the superiority of the soul over the body (cf. Ronsard, *Amours*, s.17, l.7, 'Occise aux piedz de ma fiere moitié'.) If we compare Ronsard, *Amours*, s.191 'Ren-moy mon cuœur, ren-moy mon cuœur, pil-larde' we will see how Louise Labé transposes a commonplace theme. Merrill and Clements say, in *Platonism in French Renais-sance Poetry*,

> Major French poets after Héroët's day tended to con-sider the story of the Androgyne rather as an idealising

justification of physical union than as an illustration of the lofty intellectual and spiritual ascesis which was set forth chiefly in Plato's *Symposium* and *Phaedrus*, and which became under the mediating influence of Ficino the Renaissance doctrine of Platonic love.[9]

The same authors point to the loss of deep interest as the idea becomes accepted.

The tercets look forward hopefully to reunion, and ask that it will not be 'dangereuse' (the word has been called forth by 'hazart'); the danger lies in the fact that the first meeting could create a deeper separation than absence had done, if the lover is too hard on her. Although she wants to see him she is apprehensive, a little frightened of him, because his continued coldness, without the excuse of absence, would hurt her more than her present state of uncertainty. In l.2 'de grace amiable' reminds us of the beginning of the second *Élégie*:

D'un tel vouloir le serf point ne desire
La liberté, ou son port le navire,
Comme j'atens, helas, de jour en jour
De toy, Ami, le gracieus retour.

[The slave does not long for liberty, or the ship for port so much as I, alas, wait day after day, beloved, for your kind and loving homecoming.]

In l.13 'me rende' includes the two senses, 'give me back your beauty' and 'make your beauty favourable'. It is also possible to read the last two lines either as a wish or as the fulfilment of a wish. 'Ta beauté' tells us that it is her impossible longing for his physical presence which is the reason why she considers him to be cruel. In a sense she is not exactly blaming him for his cruelty; she is so concerned about the meeting which she longs for that she is ready to take the blame for the differences between them.

SONNET 8

This sonnet is very much in the Petrarchan tradition, with its antitheses of living and dying, hot and cold. It is, in fact, so clearly within the tradition that there is not much point in trying to find sources for the contrasts. (For the sake of illustration, perhaps we could compare Ronsard, *Amours*, s.*12*, ll.1–2 'J'espère et crains, je me tais et supplie,/ Or je suis glace et ores un feu chault . . .' [I hope and fear, am silent and beseech, Now I am ice and now again hot fire . . .]). But I think that it would be a mistake to consider that the poem was bad for this reason. The poem is part of the whole sequence, and therefore is usually to be read after the passionate sensuality of s.*5* and the meditative s.*7*: on its own it may not be a good poem, but it is perhaps redeemed by the broader context, and secondly, after the very ordinary quatrains the poem does develop in an unexpected and quite original way in the tercets. Furthermore, to a modern reader, not familiar with the vast body of Petrarchan poetry in the Renaissance, the triteness cannot be so striking.

As I have already suggested, the use of traditional material, besides being part of the accepted way of writing poetry at the time, is certainly conscious in Louise Labé; here she links her collection of poems with the literary tradition but without the dull insistence that we find, for example, in the *Olive* of Du Bellay, or the Cassandre poems of Ronsard.

The contrasts which she uses in this poem fit well into her poetry of violent emotion, absolutes and extremes. The first words here, ('Je vis, je meurs') refer back to and sum up the preceding sonnet, with its initial contrast of life and death which lies behind the whole poem; 'brule' ties together all the earlier references to burning ('ardre', *2*.11, 'son feu', *4*.2, 'brulay', *4*.3, 'ardent', *4*.8, and so on) and 'noye' brings together all the equal and opposite references to 'larmes' and 'pleurs', especially the 'baignera' of *5*.7. In l.2 'estreme' is another of the words expressing absoluteness and complete-ness; it is perhaps a traditional word in the context, but ties in well with what we have already seen, and what we shall later see, of the uncompromising and relentless passion to which Louise is prey. In 'endurant froidure' the internal rhyme stresses three elements, coldness, hardness and duration. In the next line 'molle' reminds us of the previous mention of 'mon lit mol'. This is important, because for us, in the context of these poems, the association is one of frustration at the absence of the lover, which is not a sufficient contrast with 'dure' since the main reason why life is hard is his very absence. We can only conclude that the present sonnet refers to some earlier time, when she was able to enjoy the lover's presence. This is the only possible explanation of words like 'molle', 'joye', 'ris' and 'plaisir'. 'Joye' is, in fact, mentioned here for the first time, though it has already been hinted at. In this poem it is far from being the dominant emotion; it is however one that has at least an equal place in the whole sequence. The words used here to express joy must refer to some earlier experience; it is not sufficient that they should merely contrast her present joyful wishful thinking with her present unhappiness. It seems to me that she is either contrasting her present unhappiness with her former happiness, or is describing totally the past experience in which she went from the extreme of joy to the extreme of sorrow. There is a direct link between her present and past experience in 'je ris' which recalls the remembered laughter of the lover, 'Ô ris, ô front' (*2.9*). (In the third *Élégie* (l.99) it is the lover, 'Qui seul me peut faire plorer et rire' [Who alone can make me weep and laugh.])

In ll.6–7 there is further play on the word 'dure'; 'J'endure' varies the part of the verb ('endurant') and its position in the line, and 'il dure' substitutes a verb for an adjective ('trop dure') of unrelated meaning. It is of course possible that there was a momentary ambiguity in the 'trop dure' of l.3, one of its meanings being the same as 'il dure' (cf. for a similar use of these rhymes, Scève, *Délie*, *102*).

'Bien' (l.7) is a word which appears frequently in French sixteenth-century love-poetry. It can be either purely spiritual, e.g., Scève, *Délie*, *133*, ll.5–6:

> Lors ie sentis distiler en mon ame
> Le bien du bien, qui tout aultre surmonte,
> [Then I felt the highest good which surpasses all others distilled within my soul]

or it can refer to sexual fulfilment, e.g., Scève, *Délie*, *41*: (ll.1–4):

> Le veoir, l'ouyr, le parler, le toucher
> Finoient le but de mon contentement,
> Tant que le bien, qu'Amantz ont sur tout cher,
> N'eust oncques lieu en nostre accointement,
> [Seeing, hearing, speaking, touching, were the entire object of my pleasure, while the good which Lovers prize above all others, never took place in our relationship.]

or, as in the present instance, can be a mixture of both, or simply the opposite of 'mon mal'. Here the dominant note is physical (cf. 'plaisir' in the preceding line). 'A jamais il dure' presents a certain amount of difficulty. It seems to suggest spiritual fulfilment, though as we shall see this is almost entirely lacking in these sonnets. Or is it perhaps intensity (rather than eternity) of duration, making the present moment timeless? In l.8 'je seiche et je verdoye', both vivid and concrete words, however banal the images may be, continue the subtle analogy between the poet and the rest of nature. Cotgrave has, for *verdoyer*: 'To flourish; to be greene, young, lustie, youthfull, strong'; and for *seicher*: 'To dry, drayne of moisture; parch or wither; pine or wast away'. The poet is not really concerned to appeal to nature to support her in her misfortunes, nor is she interested in describing the natural setting of her experience. The images are simple and controlled.

The almost aphoristic l.9 takes us back to the similar expressions in s.*4* (ll.1 and 9); cf., also, *Élégie* I, ll.112–13,

> Ainsi Amour prend son plaisir, à faire
> Que le veuil d'un soit à l'autre contraire.
> [So love takes pleasure in ensuring that the desire of one is opposed to the other.]

In the tercets the movement (upward, onward, downward) and the variation in the speed make the poem achieve something after its unoriginal beginning. Line 9 sums up both the quatrains, and in advance, the tercets; it is Love which is in control throughout ('me meine') in spite of its apparent capriciousness. In l.12 there is a rapid ascending movement, culminating in 'certeine', though with a momentary pause on the less than absolute 'croy', which rhymes internally with 'joye' (same line) and links with the rhymes of ll.1–8; there is a sustained intensity on the plateau of l.13, then a falling movement in the last line which shows how illusory was the climax. In 'Il me remet' the god of Love is almost equated with the lover, and 'remet' introduces the alternating, almost cyclical (remet) nature of the experience. In her account of her apparent fulfilment and subsequent frustration it is the pain which stays with us, in spite of the multiple reference to 'joye'; we are left with a strong sense of the 'lacrymae rerum'.

SONNET 9

This is a sonnet of which the beginning is not at all trite, even the apparent padding of the first three words conveys immediacy and a certain inevitability. Ronsard, also, uses 'Tout aussitôt' as a correlative to 'aussi tôt que' (cf. *Amours*, s.*95*). We have already had all the words and ideas of l.2, but there is variation in the repetition: 'Le mol lit' is, strangely, more personal and intimate than 'mon lit mol'. Since the adjective 'desiré' comes after the noun, there is an immediate contrast with 'mon desiré heur' of *8*.13. In l.3 'mon triste esprit' picks up again the main theme of s.*8*, and 'hors de moy retiré' takes us back to s.*6*. There is also perhaps the suggestion of the Platonic idea of the soul being imprisoned in the body. In the present sonnet, however, she does not attempt to carry on the image of s.*6*. I do not think that Louise Labé wishes to make a distinction here between 'esprit' and 'ame', but it is possible for us to analyze more closely the different 'faculties'. Saulnier shows how in Scève 'esprit' is sometimes synonymous with 'ame', sometimes is 'the most eminent aspect of it, reasonable reflection which, by means of the senses, transmits its orders to the heart, and governs the movements of the body'; he sees it as synonymous with thought, or thinking, and as including understanding which is one of its functions, 'the creative function, and Memory, its imaginative or reproductive function'.[10] Although perhaps the poet was not exactly aware that this was the sense in which she was using 'esprit', Saulnier's definition fits this context admirably. 'Esprit' would be her imagination reaching out to the lover, and achieving this especially by the power of her memory of what the lover was like. (It is worthy of note that at the time 'esprit' or 'esperit' was almost always an equivalent of the Latin 'animus' whereas 'ame' translated 'anima'.) Sonnet *6* had equated her soul and the lover; here, in 'mon triste esprit', it is made clear that she still retains her own personality and individuality. 'Retiré' indicates violent and involuntary separation, due to some external force. In l.4 's'en va' echoes *8*.7 'mon bien s'en va'; this technique of self-quotation in consecutive sonnets is frequent in this poet and makes for greater continuity. Recent poems, and indirectly more distant poems, are thus closely linked. This line 4 is striking also because the words become almost inseparable from each other; it is scarcely possible to say which words go together according to strict syntactic patterns. The result is that the time becomes a vivid present and the line moves with rapidity. 'Se rendre' means simply 'go', but also, especially because of the falling rhythm and the strong break after the word, 'surrender'. As far as it is possible to work this sort of thing out from the dictionaries, it seems in fact, that the principal meaning at the time was the one contained in the military metaphor, and that the idea of mere movement, and of the surrender of the woman to the man were secondary. Estienne has many examples, which are either military 'Se rendre a son ennemi, Tradere se; Se rendre comme vaincu, Palmam dare; se rendre du tout soubject à ung homme, Se alicui homini addicere'; or rather more general, 'Se rendre à la merci d'aucun, soubs l'asseurance par luy promise, In fidem alicujus venire'; finally, there is an example very similar to the one in our text, 'Je me ren à toy, Dedo me tibi'. Compare also Magny *Souspirs*, s.*174*, ll.1–7,

> Cessez mes yeux de plus larmes espendre,
> Et vous mon cœur de plus vous tourmenter,
> Car celle là qui nous fait lamenter
> S'en vient vers moy pitoyable se rendre.
> [Cease weeping, my eyes, and you my heart, cease tormenting yourself, for she who causes us to lament is coming to give herself up to me in her mercifulness.]

'Je tiens le bien' is a clear back-reference to *8*.7, and is here physical (though, of course, illusory). Throughout the quatrains, the verbs, coming at the end of the lines, carry weight. Although 'desiré', 'aspiré' and 'soupiré' are all past participles they contain an idea of lack of fulfilment, which is what the whole poem is about. This sonnet relies heavily, for the speed at which it moves, on the way the lines run into each other (1/2,3/4,5/6,7/8 and 12/13/14 which is particularly strong).

'Ô dous sommeil' is an abbreviated quotation of *5*.10 'De dous repos et de sommeil espris'. 'Ô nuit à moy heureuse!' may strike us as rather odd after *5*.14. 'Crier me faut mon mal toute la nuit'. The explanation must lie in something else that we have seen already, the presence of irreconcilable elements in her poetry, and in her optimism in spite of her sufferings. Furthermore, in this present poem it is obvious that she has serious doubts about the happiness which the night and its dreams can bring. Lines 9–10 are partly ironical; neither 'plaisant' nor 'tranquilité' could possibly be appropriate words in her case. It is true that until the last word of the last line her statement is straightforward and must be taken as such, but since the tercets build up to this word we cannot ignore its force. The last tercet leaves open the question whether the wish contained in ll.12–13 will ever be fulfilled, but there is a suggestion that fulfilment is unlikely to take place.

In 'ma povre ame amoureuse' she shows that she does not always equate her soul and her lover as in s.7. Here it means simply 'I'.

This polarity between 'verité' and 'mensonge' is one which is found throughout Renaissance poetry. The near identity here of sound between 'mon songe' and 'mensonge' is telling. In spite of the desire for fulfilment in the world of dreams, 'mensonge' is her last word. 'Songe' brings inevitably with it realization *and* frustration.

The 'songe' theme is not, of course, original in Louise Labé, though she handles it very well: cf. Ronsard, *Amours*, s.*30*, ll.13–14 'Sinon d'effect, seuffre au moins que par songe /Toute une nuict je les [i.e. ces flancz] puisse embrasser'. [If not in reality, let me at least in dream, embrace your body one whole night long.]

SONNET 10

For Luc van Brabant this is one of the most important sonnets for the proof that the lover was Henri II, though he is well aware that other critics have thought it was addressed to some other unnamed poet. His main reasons seem to be that Olivier de Magny in his *Souspirs* (*88*) says that 'princes et Roys' 'de laurier ont le chef couronné', that Brantôme says that Henri liked playing the lute, and that the praise in the poem is too exaggerated for a poet but not for someone of royal rank. The evidence seems inconclusive. Giudici points to Ronsard's 'Quand j'aperçoy ton beau chef jaunissant', *Amours*, s.*66* which it seems Louise Labé must have known. (It is only, however, the first line which is parallel). Perhaps the reference in her sonnet here is after all literary rather than sentimental. In general, the first quatrain shows little more than that the lover was a successful poet (or even perhaps successful only at persuading her?)

The myth of Orpheus was popular at the time:[11] cf. *Le
débat*: 'C'estoit la douceur de sa Musique, que lon dit avoir
adouci les Loups, Tigres, Lions: attiré les arbres, et amolli
les pierres: et quelle pierre ne s'amolliroit entendant le dous
preschement de celui qui amiablement la veut atendrir pour
recevoir l'impression de bien et honneur?' [It was the sweetness of his music, that is said to have made wolves, tigers
and lions gentle; to have attracted trees and softened stones:
and what stone would not soften, hearing the sweet preaching
of the one who in his kindness wants to soften it, for it to
receive an impression of goodness and honour.]

The structure of the quatrains ('Quand . . . quand . . .
Lors . . .') recalls that of s.*9*, ('Tout aussi tot . . . Lors . . .').
'D'un laurier verd' traditionally signified renown or fame,
especially that of poets. Petrarch had given the idea even
wider currency in his singing of Laura and his play on the
words 'lauro (l'auro)' and 'laura (l'aura)'. Maurice Scève,
and the followers of Petrarch in France had also used the
words and the idea. 'Faire un Lut si bien pleindre' takes us
back to s.*2*; in both sonnets the incantatory and melancholic
seductiveness of the lover's playing is alluded to. The great
Orphic power which he has over her is brought out in the
contrast between 'arbres et rocs' and the immediately following 'quand je te vois'. She implies without actually stating it
that she is unable to resist his persuasiveness. The point of
this long sentence comes in l.11: 'Why can't such excellence
(vertus) make *you* love *me*?' This is a subtle reference to the
last tercet of s.*2*:

> De toy me plein, que tant de feus portant,
>
> En tant d'endrois d'iceus mon cœur tatant,
>
> N'en est sur toy volé quelque estincelle.

The inversion in ll.4–5 is not successful because it makes
the sentence unnecessarily padded and the syntax involved;
it seems to be used for metrical reasons only. The close link
between the quatrains is intended to give movement and
continuity—there is no reason at all why the poem should not
consist of a single sentence of fourteen lines but here the
thread is in danger of being lost. 'Plus haut que nul' is an
intensive comparison, typical of the poet, but is cumbersome

in the context. 'Chef d'honneur' in l.6 appears to refer (but does not do so) to 'ton blond chef'; the repetition is confused and adds nothing to the poem.

After these seven lines of subordinate clauses, the link 'Lors' seems at first too strong, until we realize that it introduces not a short concluding 'pointe' but further involved clauses. There is much weakness in this part of the poem, for example, the double repetition of 'vertus' (though it is true that in l.12 'vertu' has a different meaning from 'vertus' in l.9); line 10 is a feeble repetition of l.9, though there is good off-beat balance in the position of 'te font estre' in each line.

In l.13 'nom' means 'reputation' and thus links with 'laurier verd' (cf. *Élégie* 11, ll.56–7, where Louise talks of her reputation (renom)). In the last line 'enflamer' depends on 'pour-roient' (l.11). 'Doucement' contrasts with 'passionné' (l.8), for which Estienne gives the synonym 'hors de soymesmes', and Cotgrave has: 'Passioned, passionate, perturbed, much distempered, or troubled in mind; off the hindges, almost distraught, well-nigh besides himselfe'.

SONNET 11

The first line of this sonnet is similar to 2.1, 'Ô beaus yeus bruns, ô regars destournez' and it is possible that the 'dous regars' may explain the earlier 'regars destournez' as averted through shyness rather than through disdain: more immed-iately 'dous' recalls the wish at the end of s.*10*, 'De mon amour doucement t'enflamer', and, beyond this, 'Qui doucement me rende ta beauté/ . . . favorable' of *7*.13–14.

The poem contrasts the two faces of love, the delightfully idyllic moments of attraction by the senses (especially that of sight), and the painful effect it has on her. The imagery of the first quatrain is consciously trite. She is here playing with the language of love.

'Les flesches dangereuses' has a double resonance: firstly there is the obvious reference to the whole tradition of the arrows of love and their association with the eyes (cf. 'nouveaus dars', *3*.10, etc.,), and then there is the reference to s.*7*, 'que ne soit dangereuse/Cette rencontre . . .' We may compare Ronsard, *Amours* s.*41*, ll.1–4 'Ha, Seigneur dieu, que de graces écloses/Dans le jardin de ce sein verdelet,/

Enflent le rond de deus gazons de lait,/Où des Amours les fléches sont encloses!' [Ah, Lord God, what delights, unfolded in the garden of this young breast, plump out the roundness of two milky lawns, where the arrows of Love are enclosed.] (Weber, ed. *Amours*, p.522, sees this passage as a conflation of two from Ariosto.) In l.4 'Tant' should be taken with 's'est arresté', 'has spent so long in . . .', 'has dwelt so long . . .'

The second quatrain returns to the theme of the cruelty of love, and, as in s.7, it is beauty which calls forth cruelty, and not just for the sake of the rhyme. 'Ô rude cruauté' is a subtle variation on 'Ô cruautez, ô durtez inhumaines' (3.5). 'Felon' had several meanings at the time according to Huguet: 'cruel, méchant, farouche/violent, furieux/fier, ardent, fort/qui fait cruellement souffrir'. In all this there does not seem to be the meaning of 'treacherous' or 'traitorous', which it had earlier and later. Cotgrave has: *'felon.* Fell; fellonious; furious, despightfull, cruell, curst, pitiless, harsh, rough, froward, untractable, outragious', and gives the proverb 'Amour vainc tout fors, que le cœur felon' [Love conquers any thing but a fellonious heart]. In l.6 'Tant tu me tiens' takes us back to 'Je tiens le bien' which comes in exactly the same place in the sonnet in 9.6. The phrases are contrasted: in the one she claims (though it is not entirely true) that she possesses love, in the other (which is true) that she is possessed by love. 'Façons' means here both 'fantaisie, caprice' (Huguet) and it contains, as did so many words at the time derived from the Latin words 'facere' and 'fingere' the idea of deception. It points again to the illusory nature of loving possession. The rhyme 'amoureuses/dangereuses', etc., common enough in other poets, is also one used already in this sequence (s.7): this is not a defect but another way of linking the sonnets by partially rhyming them with each other.

In the tercets 'Donques', again, does not denote a strict logical conclusion but merely provides the transition. 'Plaisir' echoes immediately 'plaisant repos' (9.10) and 'plaisir' (8.6), and 'tours' echoes, in part, 'tourmentez'; the whole phrase 'tant de bons tours' recalls 'd'un bon tour' in 6.5.

The last four lines contain an almost allegorical account of a personified encounter between her eyes and her heart, and take us back to the interplay between 'ame', 'esprit' and 'cœur' in s.8 and s.10. This technique reminds us of similar

passages in the dizains of Scève's *Délie*. There is some confusion in Louise Labé: in l.7 it is the eyes which produce
'larmes langoureuses', whereas in l.12 'languiz' refers to the
heart. The struggle seems to be that the sight of her beloved
always makes her want him, whereas her heart makes her
feel pain, and promises future pain (l.13). In ll.11–12
('plus . . . plus . . . plus') the comparison makes for quick
movement and great intensity. 'Souci' stands out and is the
keynote of this otherwise pretty poem.

The last two lines are cut off from the rest by their meaning.
'Devinez' is addressed both to the eyes and to the reader
directly. 'Si je suis aise aussi' jars a little at first: in Louise
Labé the 's' sound (and especially in this combination, with
these vowels) usually denotes sensuality and peacefulness.
Here it is the opposite she wants to stress; she is *not* 'aise'.
Or is she perhaps trying to show her sensual experience even
of this emotion, and so stress her disturbance at the conflict
between eye and heart?

SONNET 12

This sonnet, directly addressed to the poet's lute (unlike s.*2*
which merely invokes it), has been taken by Luc van Brabant
as the dividing line between the sonnets inspired by Henri II
and those inspired by Olivier de Magny (though Henri will
reappear in s.*19* which is placed where it is because of the
time of composition); s.*12* would then be a summary or
recapitulation of the preceding sonnets. There may be some
truth in this, though my own impression is that Van Brabant's
arguments are often circular.

We have come to associate the lute with the *lover's* power
to charm; here it is her own lute she is addressing in order to
emphasize her loneliness, in the same way as in s.*5* she had
said 'De ses travaus voyant témoins tes yeus' to convey her
solitude. Because of its position in the line, and in the poem,
'De mes soupirs' recalls 'O chaus soupirs' (*2*.2) and 'Tristes
soupirs' (*3*.2). 'Irreprochable' introduces a moral idea, but
the word does not carry great weight. (The lute is a true
witness, is always present at her troubles, and cannot lie. In
the same way, therefore, since lute stands for poetry, her
poetry is a true and complete record).*

'Controlleur' presents some difficulty. 'Contrerolleur', as it was usually written at the time, is a figurative use of a word which was principally employed in matters of finance. (Estienne gives, 'Antigraphus Officij exactor, Custos, Obseruator'). In the present poem there is the general sense of 'observer' (cf., 'témoin'), but there is also the idea of 'teller' or 'accountant'. Cotgrave has much to say about *Contrerolle* and *Contrerolleur: contrerolle* is 'A controlement, or contrarolement; the copie of a roll, (of accounts &c.) a Paralell of the same qualitie and content, with th' originall; also, a controlling, or overseeing; and th'Office of a Controller, or overseer; also, a Controler, or overseer', and *contrerolleur* is 'A Controller; observer, overseer; properly, an Officer, that takes notes, or keepes a roll, of another Officers accounts, thereby to discover him if he do amisse'. He goes on to list 'Contrerolleurs des Aides, de l'Audience de France, des Chanceleries, du Domaine, des finances,' and so on. It is worth noting that a synonym of 'Contrerolleur' is sometimes 'Secretaire': this sense would fit in well, in Louise Labé, with 'compagnon' and 'témoin', and the whole Petrarchan tradition. 'Veritable' partly echoes 'Ne doit avoir de bien en verité' (*9*.13) but there is no need to look more closely for a particular significance. 'Tu as souvent avec moy lamenté' refers both to incidents in her own past experience of love, and also to the experience which we have had vicariously in the poems we have read so far; the perfect tense carries through clearly into the present. At the end of the first quatrain 'lamenté' rhymes with 'tourmenté' in the preceding sonnet, thus making a link in sound and meaning between the two.

The second quatrain shows the very close, almost reciprocal, relationship between herself and her lute. In l.6, the subject of 'commençant' is not clear; is it the poet herself, or perhaps 'le pleur piteus' of l.5, which, of course, stands for her, or is it the lute? Whichever it is, it seems certain that the subject in l.8 must be 'le pleur piteus'. 'Tout soudein' expresses the violent change of situation (especially involuntary) of which Louise Labé is so fond; (cf. *8*.5 'Tout à un coup' and *9*.1 'Tout aussi tot'). 'Feignant' is a very common word in the arts of poetry written in the middle of the sixteenth century, and in the numerous poems written about the writing of poetry. It is not always clear whether it means simply to make or to imitate (without any pejorative sense), or as here to simulate, even to counterfeit.

The tercets develop the theme of the lute and the lutanist. Critics have not all agreed about the meaning of l.9, and some have even amended the original text to 'Et si tu veus'. There does not seem to be any necessity for this; in any case, if that is the correct meaning it would be equally well conveyed by the original text, because the omission of the pronoun is quite usual. Normally, 's'efforcer' is used reflexively, but there are a few instances where it is used as a transitive verb. Cotgrave does not give *efforcer* but has: '*S'efforcer*. To indevor, labour, inforce himselfe; to strive with might and maine; to use his utmost strength, apply all his vigour, imploy his whole power'. Palsgrave gives: 'I take a woman agaynst her wyll. *Je force une femme*, prim. conj. What meanest thou, man, wylt thou take me agaynst my wyl: *que veulx tu dire, me veulx tu efforcer?*' Here then the text would mean 'Si je te veus' and not 'si tu te veus' because this gives far better sense. 'Au contraire' refers back to the antithesis in *11*.14. 'à mon cœur contraire', and 'contreins' to *10*.3 'à te suivre contreindre'. 'Tu te destens' is to be taken literally (Estienne gives 'Destendre les cordes de quelque instrument de musique, Neruos remittere' and nothing else, and in any case the figurative sense would not fit in here). 'Me voyant' and 'Donnant' seem to need 'toy' as their subject, but the construction is odd, since then the second participle would stand instead of a finite verb, 'tu donnes'.

There are many internal rhymes and repetitions within this poem working harmoniously towards a description of the interaction between the woman and her lute: (soupirs/soupirer; témoin/moy; ennuis/ennuis; lamenté/lamentable; rendois/destens/tendrement; contraire/contreins/contreinte; plein/pleinte).

In the last tercet we see that she delights in her pain, though this is something to which she is driven. Her usual mood is not one in which she is able to talk of 'dous mal', in spite of the fact that this was part of the literary tradition (cf. Ronsard, *Amours*, s.*46*, ll.1-2, 'Amour me tue, et si je ne veus dire/Le plaisant mal que ce m'est de mourir' . . . [Love is killing me, and yet I will not say what pleasant pain this dying is.]) and does appear in s.*11*; the 'douce fin' which she hopes for is a commonplace in this kind of poetry, and points to total physical and personal release.

Giudici takes exception to Harvey's division of many of the sonnets.[12] In this one, instead of dividing 10/4 he would prefer 4/4/4/2. It is not easy to resolve this sort of question, but it seems clear to me that there is a more important pause after the quatrains than after l.10. Compare, on the same theme as the present sonnet, *Délie, 344*.

SONNET 13

This is one of the sonnets usually found in anthologies, because of its obvious and undeniable merit; it is even greater in its place in the sequence than as an independent poem. Its two most striking characteristics are its sensuality and its movement, from the first passionate 'Oh' to the culmination of happiness in the last word 'heureuse'. The whole poem is written as a kind of wish, and expresses desire very vividly. It has none of the bitterness and frustration of the 'songe' theme (cf. s.*9*) though there are some structural parallels. Here the conditional is fulfilled.

'Ravie' to the sixteenth-century ear was often associated with 'fureur' (cf. note on *4*.3). 'En ce beau sein . . ./De celui là pour lequel' seems at first pleonastic, but it is only the 'ce' which is intrusive, and in any case there is a development: l.2 is a further explanation either to herself or to the reader. This use of syntax is good, pointing emphatically, intimately. 'En ce beau sein' answers 'mon sein tendre' (*9*.5) in the same way as their eyes and hearts reply to each other throughout the sonnets. In the second line here 'mourant' brings in another of the themes of this poem, that of life and death, which is expressed both by means of direct statement and by the presence of the rhymes in 'vie', especially 'en/vie'.

'De mes cours jours' is a variant on the 'carpe diem' theme so common in Renaissance poetry, and by its sound the phrase links with 'tours' and 'retours'. 'Envie' has many meanings in sixteenth-century French: Huguet gives 'haine, colère, mécontentement', though it certainly could also mean 'desire' or 'wish', and very frequently, especially in love poetry, meant 'jealousy'. Cotgrave has: 'Envy, spight, grudge, repining; griefe, displeasure at the prosperitie, or good parts of another; a malicious emulation; also, a desire, or lust unto, a longing after'. In the present poem it stands for any evil force, but more particularly, jealousy personified as the disrupter of happy love-affairs.

In the second quatrain, since there are no quotation marks in the original text, editors have put them in different places, beginning before 'chere' and ending either after 'l'autre' or after 'vie'. It seems to me that the passage makes better sense if we include ll.7–8 in the inverted commas, rather than making 's'asseurant' equivalent to 'm'acollant'. 'S'asseurant' does not simply refer to the lover, but because of the reciprocity of 'contentons nous' the 'se' contains the 'nous'. The word expresses her confidence and trust in the protective power of the lover.

The poem moves swiftly, because l.5 looks forward to what the lover goes on to say in the next line, and because of the enjambement in ll.6–7. There is indeed a close parallel between the way in which 's'asseurant' leads into the next line, and the effect of 'le demeurant' at the end of l.3, even though they are not grammatically equivalent. 'Ja' (cf. modern French 'déjà') means 'now' or 'henceforth'.

'Euripe' is perhaps to us a recondite allusion. It is the narrow channel between Euboea and Boetia, famous for its turbulent currents. To the sixteenth-century reader, however, it was almost a commonplace; the poets used it frequently, imitating Livy and Lucan. Du Bellay, for example, in his *Ode au Reverendiss. Cardinal du Bellay*, writes,

> Cetuy la qui s'estudie / Representer en ses vers
> Tous les accidens divers / De l'humaine tragedie,
> Celuy encores descrive / Tous les floz tumultueux
> Qui retournent à la rive / D'Euripe l'impetueux.[13]

> [He who endeavours to depict in his verses all the various accidents of the human tragedy, let him describe also all the tumultuous waves which return to the shore of impetuous Euripus.]

Torrentin has: 'Euripus . . . est pars maris inter Euboiam et Boëtiam, ubi fluctus septies in die et toties in nocte mutatur tam uehementer, ut naues plenis uelis currentes retrahat secum, accipitur pro quouis fluctu'. Calepin, on the other hand, says 'unius diei et noctis spatio septies recurrit eo

impetu, ut nauigia, repugnantibus ventis plena secum rapiat'.
['Euripus which is that part of the sea between Euboea and
Boetia, where the tide changes seven times each day and as
many times each night so violently that it drags with it ships
in full sail, is taken to stand for any strong flood'; 'in the space
of one day and night it flows back seven times with such force
that it drags ships in full sail against the wind'.] Louise Labé
refers to it again, herself, in *Le débat*: 'Aristote ne mourut il
de dueil, comme un fol, ne pouvant entendre la cause du flus
et reflus de l'Euripe ?' [Didn't Aristotle die of grief and madness because he couldn't understand what caused the ebb and
flow of the Euripus ?]

In the first tercet we find another absolute use of the present
participle, since 'tenant' refers to Louise and the subject of
the sentence is 'la mort'. 'Le tenant acollé' is a powerful
variation on 'acollant', giving greater strength and permanence to the embrace. The image of ivy clinging to the tree
was a commonplace to describe the union of lovers. Line 9 is
successful because 'encercelé' encloses it both in meaning and
structurally. The next line takes up the question of death
already mentioned in 'vois mourant', but the idea is now
literal instead of figurative. The later line makes 'vois mourant'
more actual and concrete in retrospect. 'Envieuse' takes up
'envie' and explains it further; Cotgrave gives: 'Envious,
malignant, repining, despightfull, spighting, at another mans
worth, or fortune'. Death is one of the forces of evil which are
working to destroy her. (Perhaps also this adds another
dimension to the 'Quelque menasse et procheine ruïne/
Quelque penser de mort qui tout termine' of *4*.6–7). 'Mon aise'
recalls *11*.13 'si je suis aise aussi'.

Until l.10 the movement of the sonnet has been fast, but
there is a reflective pause in ll.11–13. 'Lors que' is still part
of the conditional clause begun in the first line; since this
phrase is introduced by 'lors que' and not by 'si' the phrase
appears more vivid and real for being dwelt on. 'Souef' is
another adverb used as an adjective (cf. 'incontinent' in *9*.4),
and emphasizes the sensuality by its relative unusualness.
'Baiseroit', in a sense, has been called for by 'aise' (the two
words were often rhymed together). Line 13 recalls *9*.3–4,
'Mon triste esprit, hors de moy retiré'. The idea of the soul
being taken out of the body by a kiss, was fairly common, as

also was the idea of the death-bringing kiss; cf. Ronsard, *Amours*, s.*80*, ll.1–4:

'Si je trépasse entre tes bras, Madame,/Il me suffit, car je ne veus avoir/Plus grand honneur, sinon que de me voir/En te baisant, dans ton sein rendre l'ame' [If I die within your arms, my lady, that will satisfy me for I do not wish to have greater honour than breathing my last while kissing you.], and cf. also s.*209*, ll.9–14. Weber points out[14] that Ronsard is here developing the theme of the kiss after Jean Second, which he had used in the *Odes* (11), dedicated to Cassandre, in 1550.

After the repeated 'si' clauses, 'Bien' in the last line, gives a simple yet forceful conclusion. The last line is to be understood, 'Then shall I die, happier than if I were still alive'. Giudici notes another possible interpretation 'happier than any other living person', and rejects it, because of its flatness, though otherwise it would fit in. He says of this sonnet that it is 'almost a moment of folly, of forgetfulness, of drunkenness: not the slow, calm abandon of the twelfth sonnet but a different kind of abandon, a forgetting of everything in view of the supreme Good, Love, a complete annihilation of her own entire being in the unique reality of passion.'[15]

SONNET 14

As we begin reading this sonnet we have still echoing in our ears the emphatic 'Bien je mourrois' of sonnet 13. The present sonnet, too, turns out to be about death, but the tone has changed from one of predominant optimism to one of pessimism. The echo of the previous sonnet adds depth to this one.

The tense of the first line ('pourront') gains from its similarity to 'mourrois' while being significantly different from it. The future denotes continuity and certainty without absolute permanence. 'Larmes espandre' takes us back to the 'larmes espandues' of *2*.2 and carries this idea through the present into the future.

There is a near ambiguity of sound in 'l'heur passé'; the meaning is 'happiness' but 'l'heure' (time) is not far away. As in *9*.4, l.2 gains force because of our uncertainty which words are to be taken together. 'Avec toy' can be taken either with 'passé' or with 'regretter'; 'regretter' itself, it should be noted, has different meanings in French and English. In French it often means 'miss' rather than 'be sorry for', or 'repent of'. In the sixteenth century the principal meaning seems to have been the idea of longing for, or missing something, though the sense of 'repenting' also existed. The first meaning given in the Estienne dictionary is 'Regretter *aucun*, Capere desyderium ex aliquo, Desyderio alicuius moueri, Requirere'; in the same way, in Du Bellay's Latin poem 'Desiderium Patriae' the word 'Desiderium' is synonymous with the word 'Regret' which is the title of his nostalgic Roman poems. Huguet gives 'se lamenter sur, plaindre'. Palsgrave gives: 'I make mone, I complyne me for a losse or that I am out of presence of them that I love. *Je me regrete.* . . .' Cotgrave, for his part, has: 'To desire, affect, wish for, looke or long after; also, to bewayle, bemoane, lament, grieve, sorrow, repent, for' and for *Regret*: 'Desire, will, affection, stomacke, or humor unto; also, griefe, sorrow, repentance, forthinking'. 'Passé', incidentally, recalls a favourite series of words in Louise Labé (cf. lassée, assez, cassée). In l.3 'aus sanglots et soupirs', which is an utterly traditional sort of phrase in this kind of writing manages nonetheless to hold some interest for us because of the way in which it reminds us of 'j'ay si haut souspiré/Que de sanglots . . .' of *9.*7–8.

'Les cordes tendre' contains both 'Tu te destens' (*12.*10) and 'tendre' in the meaning of 'tender', though of course there is no real ambiguity here. 'Mignart' is a stock, semi-precious epithet in the poets of the time (especially Baïf and Belleau). 'L'esprit' (l.7) is clearly 'mon esprit' (following 'mes yeus', 'ma voix', 'ma main'). 'Comprendre' is rich in resonances. It means at once 'grasp, seize, embrace and understand' (Cotgrave gives: 'To comprehend, containe, comprise, compasse; to perceive, understand, apprehend, attaine unto the knowledge of; to conceive, to be capable of'), and expresses total involvement.

The power of the quatrains is due to the fact that they do not contain a main verb, but look forward, at this stage optimistically, to the future continuation of present happiness. They express a near eternity of duration. Line 9 therefore is all the more emphatic since it carries the quatrains through into the tercets and then stops abruptly, stressing that she has no desire for death as long as she remembers her past love, and is able to love and show her love in the present. It is important to note that l.9 means 'I do not wish to die' and not 'I wish not to die' which would have come as a conclusion to the quatrains. As it is, l.9 looks forward to ll.10–14 and especially to l.14. Here the parallel to *13*.14 is evident, but there is a different reason behind the desire for death in each case. In s.*13* there was a union of love and death, whereas here they are separate and mutually exclusive. Notice the close structural parallel between ll.1–9 and ll.10–14: 'Mais quand mes yeus' mirrors 'Tant que mes yeus', and the build-up to l.14 is the same as the build-up to l.9, with short independent clauses followed by a longer one, and then by the main clause. Lines 10–12 point clearly to the structure of the poem by the repetition of the words 'yeus, voix, main, esprit'. 'Tarir' is a reference to *3*.4 'maintes rivieres' and 'sources et fontaines'. 'Cassee' we remember from *5*.12 'Et quand je suis quasi toute cassee' which refers to the whole person and not just to the voice. In any case 'voix' means more than just voice; Cotgrave gives: 'A voyce, a sound, noise, tune, word, crie; a repercussion of th'aire; talke, bruit, report'. Here it refers to her poetry (song) itself. 'Impuissante' reminds us that the whole sequence deals with the power with which the experience of love invests her.

It reminds us also of the beginning of the first *Élégie*, when Louise says that in the first stages of her love (ll.5–6)

Encore lors je n'avois la puissance

De lamenter ma peine et ma souffrance.

[At that time I had not yet the power to lament my pain and suffering.]

In the second *Élégie*, addressed to the absent lover, Louise says that in her despair she does actually want to die (ll. 83–88):

Et n'ayant rien qui plaise à ma pensee,

De tout plaisir me treuve delaissee,

Et pour plaisir, ennui saisir me vient.

Le regretter et plorer me convient,

Et sur ce point entre un tel desconfort,

Que mile fois je souhaite la mort.

[And having nothing pleasant to think about, I find I am deprived of all pleasure; instead of pleasure, melancholy takes hold of me. Regret and lamentation suit my condi-

tion and then my wretchedness becomes so great that a
thousand times I long for death.]
'Mon plus cler jour' is an amalgam of *13*.4 'De mes cours
jours' and 'Clere Venus' (*5*.1) and 'ce cler Astre' (*6*.2).

SONNET 15

This is rather a slight poem, but it is not without its effect
since it comes after the bitter despair of s.*14*. The prettiness
of the poem shows Louise Labé in one (not very common)
mood in her writing, that of uncomplicated ease and delight.
There is in the sonnet, too, the deeper idea of renewal in
nature and in love: we might notice the presence of all four
elements in this cosmic renewal (la terre, l'air, le soleil, l'eau).
Luc van Brabant even sees it as being not about a sunrise but
about the coming of spring, and sees a reference to frost in
ll.3–6. There does not seem to be any need to accept this
interpretation since the passage can mean simply that 'le
Zephir' arouses the earth and the waters, which sleep has
kept still and dark during the night; darkness could apply
equally well to winter *or* to the night, and the waters are no
more still during winter than they are during the night.

In a sense the whole poem presents and expresses the same
kind of escapism as it is suggested that nature does, cf. l.8
'aus passans font l'ennui moderer'. There is a clear progression
from general to particular, inanimate to animate, cosmic to
personal (sun, water, flowers, birds, nymphs, humans). Obviously Louise does not talk about her own beauty in her love-
poetry, but refers to it here symbolically by means of the
flowers (her physical beauty), the birds (her singing), the
nymphs (her dancing). The point of this poem is to show that
her lover, her sun, brings out all her charms. Because of the
tone of the rest of the poems one has the impression here,
which may be no more than an impression, that she is not
taking herself seriously in this stock description of the trick-
ling streams and the flower-decked fields; one feels that she
is conscious of the tradition within which she is writing.

Lines 11–12 make explicit the point of the poem (her place
in the cycle of nature). 'Ton heur' links directly with the
previous sonnet ('l'heur passé'). Although the poem describes
an idyllic peacefulness, it is still a poem of absence, looking

forward to the return of the lover ('mon Soleil'). The last
line, because of the sixteenth-century equation of beauty and
virtue, talks of a 'provocation à mieux', a common theme in
the love-poetry. A good example of this is to be found in
Ronsard, *Amours* (1552–3), s.*95*:

> Morne de cors, et plus morne d'espris
> Je me trainoi' dans une masse morte,
> Et sans sçavoir combien la Muse aporte
> D'honneur aus siens, je l'avois à mépris:

> Mais aussi tôt, que de vous je m'épris,
> Tout aussi tôt votre œil me fut escorte
> A la vertu, voire de telle sorte
> Que d'ignorant je devin bien apris.

> Donques mon Tout, si je fai quelque chose,
> Si dignement de vos yeus je compose,
> Vous me causés vous mesmes ces effets.

> Je pren de vous mes graces plus parfaites,
> Car je suis manque, et dedans moi vous faites,
> Si je fai bien, tout le bien que je fais.

[Dull in body and still duller in spirit, I dragged out my
existence in a lifeless mass; and not knowing the honour
which the Muse brings her followers, I despised her. But
as soon as I had fallen in love with you, your eye was my
guide on the path to virtue, even to such an extent that I
exchanged my ignorance for knowledge. Therefore, my
All, if I achieve anything, if the poems I compose are
worthy of your eyes, it is you who produce these effects
in me. From you I receive my greatest accomplishments,
because I am imperfection, and if I achieve anything, it is
you who produce in me all my achievement.]

Since most love-poetry was written by men and not women,
it is usually the woman who is seen as inspiring the man to
virtue. Here Louise says that she feels she is nothing without
him, and that his presence alone will make her more beautiful.
She is well aware of the change in personality which love
can bring about, cf. *Élégie* III (ll.70–2):

> Je n'ay qu'Amour et feu en mon courage,
> Qui me desguise, et fait autre paroitre,
> Tant que ne peu moymesme me connoitre.

Héroët, in *La parfaicte amye* (l.1421) even says

Qui n'ayme point, ne scauroit estre belle.

['Fiery Love is all I have in my heart, disguising me and making me appear different, so that I can no longer recognize myself'; 'A woman who does not love cannot be beautiful'.]

The reader will make the parallel between this prayer for the return of the lover and s.*7* which mentions her apprehension at an imminent meeting. In s.*15* the mood is quite different, one of gentle excitement and anticipation.

SONNET 16

The opening lines of this sonnet have much in common with s.*13* ('tempeste, Euripe, ne Courant') where the forces of nature are similarly invoked to give a further dimension to human feelings. At a first reading of ll.1–3 we assume that the parallel to be made is that in her own relationship with her lover there will be a calm after the storm (and indeed we have already seen this in the contrast between s.*14* and s.*15*). But although this idea is certainly present, it is not the factor common to the other two parallels in ll.4–6, and ll.7–8 and the tercets, where the stress is clearly on a change of situation rather than anything else. The result is that the imagery is confused and lacks the impact which clarity would have given to it, even though the individual elements are successful.

In classical and neo-classical writing the Caucasus was often mentioned as the inhospitable terrifying abode of the giants. Torrentin merely has 'Caucasus . . . mons Scythie altissimus et longissimus, qui ab India tendit per totum ferè Septentrionem', but Calepin adds that it is 'asper et inhospitalis' and quotes Virgil, *Aeneid VI* 'sed duris genuit te cautibus horrens Caucasus'; and Charles Estienne says 'cacumina habens praerupta, perpetuisque nivibus tecta'. Scève in *Délie*, *77*, ll.1–2, has: 'Au Caucasus de mon souffrir lyé/Dedans l'Enfer de ma peine eternelle. . . .' (cf. *Délie*, *149*.) ['Caucasus . . . the highest and longest mountain of Scythia, stretching from India almost throughout the North'; 'rough and inhospitable'; 'Caucasus, bristling with rugged rocks, gave birth to you'; 'having precipitous summits, covered with perpetual snow'; 'bound on the Caucasus of my suffering, within the hell of my eternal pain'.]

'Le beau jour vient' (l.3) recalls the whole of s.*15* through the opening line 'Pour le retour du Soleil honorer'.

There is very little reference to classical mythology in Louise Labé (this is one of the characteristics by which she is distinguished from her contemporaries), and what there is is simple. She does not, however, always handle it particularly felicitously; a comparison between the quatrains and the tercets of this poem illustrates how much better she writes when she is describing her feelings directly and not through the veil of poetic fable. Phœbus is Apollo, the Sun-God; he is also the god of Poetry (cf. first *Élégie*, l.7 'Phebus, ami des Lauriers vers').

In ll.4–6 the image changes from one of calm after the storm to night following day (which recalls 2.3–4, 'Ô noires nuits . . . Ô jours luisans'). The succession of night and day is seen in cyclic terms ('son cerne'). 'A grand erre' means 'quickly'; it is apparently derived from 'errer', 'to wander'. Estienne gives, 'magnis itineribus, Celeriter, Festinanter', and Cotgrave '*Aller grand erre*, ou, *à grand erre, ou grand erres*. To speed, make hast, hy apace, goe very fast', and derives it from '*Erre*: A way, path; course, or pace'. 'Sa Seur' is Phœbe, the moon, cf. *Élégie* II, ll.49–50 'Desja deus fois depuis le promis terme / De ton retour, Phebe ses cornes ferme'. [Twice already since the promised time of your return, Phœbe has closed her horns.]

The third statement in the poem occupies ll.7–8. Again there is no immediate connection with the preceding lines, except that there is a change in situation—after fighting, the Parthian flees. More importantly, the reader does not easily see what is the link between ll.7–8 and the emotional state of the author.

Nor do the tercets really answer the quatrains, in spite of an attempt to do so by means of the link-words, 'Apres qu'un tems', 'Quand', 'Quand quelque tems' and 'Un tems'. They do, however, constitute a fine poem on their own. First of all they refer back to the earlier poems—'consolé' is a direct reference to 'l'ennui moderer' of *15*.8, and 'pleintif' recalls all the poems in which the word, in one of its forms appears, and especially 'Ô lut pleintif' (2.10), and, through this, 'Lut . . . de mes ennuis controlleur veritable' (s.*12*).

When she writes in ll.9–10 that the lover has had reason to reproach her, we may be a little surprised at her 'feu peu hatif'. By this slight anecdote (there are scarcely any incidents of her experience related in the sequence, whereas most other contemporary poets introduced 'factual' background detail) she hints at other historical details which it is not to her purpose to mention. 'Defiant' means 'distrusting' but contains also the idea of 'provoking'—Estienne gives 'prouocare' as the *only* meaning, as does Cotgrave: 'To defie, challenge, provoke, or call unto fight, or contention'.

The tercets have taken the traditional Petrarchan antithesis (such as is seen in the similar 'J'ay chaut estreme en endurant froidure' (*8*.2) and transformed it into a direct and simple account of emotional experience. The sexual meaning of ll.9–14 is clear, especially taken in conjunction with ll.7–8.

The passage of time is important in this sonnet (cf. once more the link-words) to support her changing moods. One reason why these lines are so successful is that it is rare to read in poetry about a man's coldness in love, and especially one which is greater ('Et es plus froit') than the woman's. We may compare with the last tercet, firstly *Élégie* II, ll.16–18:

> peut estre ton courage
> S'est embrasé d'une nouvelle flamme,
> En me changeant pour prendre une autre Dame:
> [perhaps your heart has been set alight by a new flame, exchanging me for another woman]

and ll.53–4,

> Si toutefois, pour estre enamouré
> En autre lieu, tu as tant demeuré . . .
> [If however you have delayed so much because you have fallen in love with someone else. . . .]

Courbet, in his edition of *Les souspirs* of Olivier de Magny (1874) p. 19, compares this sonnet with s.*175* of the *Souspirs*, as proof of the relationship between the two poets. This sonnet is worth quoting here in full, if not for its anecdotal interest, at least for its psychological relevance:

> Je ne diray iamais les causes de ma peine,
> Mais trop bien à iamais ie diray que ie suis
> Le miserable auteur de mes propres ennuys,
> Causant moy mesme en moy cette angoisse inhumaine.

Mon mal vient de mon bien, et le dueil que ie meine
Naist d'un plaisir parfait, qu'obtenir ie ne puis,
Ayant mes pauures sens si malement reduits
Qu'ilz se meurent de soif aupres de la fonteine.

J'auoy tant poursuiuy qu'on m'auoit acordé
Le bon tour que i'auoy longuement demandé,
Mais quand ce uint au point que ie le pouuoy prendre,

Je deuins impotent, et ne sçeuz faire rien,
De sorte que priuant moy-mesme de mon bien,
Je priuay mon espoir pour iamais d'y pretendre.

[I will never relate the cause of my suffering, but I will always be ready to say I am the wretched author of my own troubles, causing myself this inhuman anguish within me. My suffering springs from my happiness, and the sorrow I am undergoing comes from a perfect pleasure, which is beyond my grasp, and has reduced my poor senses to the state of dying of thirst beside the fountain. I had been so persistent in my pursuit that at last I was granted the privilege I had so long asked for, but when it came to the point that I could enjoy it, I became incapable, and unable to do anything, so that by depriving myself of my happiness, I lost the hope of ever aspiring to it again.]

SONNET 17

This sonnet is more satisfactory than the previous one, because of the unity of its theme and its compactness. Unlike most of the other sonnets in the sequence it takes account, if only briefly, of the world which is external to the lovers' experience, and at the same time shows that it is not important or relevant to them. It contains, of course, a Petrarchan commonplace; cf. Ronsard, *Nouvelle continuation des amours* (1556), s.*18*, ll.1–4: 'Les villes et les bourgs me sont si odieux / Que je meurs, si je voy quelque tracette humaine: / Seulet dedans les boys pensif je me promeine, / Et rien ne m'est plaisant que les sauvages lieux'. [Towns and cities are so odious to me that I die if I see a human trace; I walk pensively alone in the woods, and nothing pleases me except wild places.]

The initial sound ('fuis') is one which is to run through the sonnet, ('ennuieus', 'puis', 'sui'), and it recalls the previous sonnet ('fuite', 'suis'), and is a key link-sound in the sequence.

The first quatrain shows a conversational disregard for strictly logical order and correct syntax. 'Vile' is a general word which includes 'temples' (particular, but standing for all public places), and finally 'tous lieus' is the most general of all, and another illustration of Louise Labé's liking for absolute expressions. The syntax of ll.1–4 deserves some attention: 'prenant plaisir' agrees with 'me' (l.3), but since it comes before the word it goes with, there is momentary confusion, which is dissipated by 't'ouïr'. (It also, of course, goes with 'Je fuis' and looks at first as if it will introduce another phrase in the first person). There is further syntactic doubt in l.4 with 'ce qu'estimois': because of the omission of the pronoun, its subject could be either 'je' or 'tu'. (The translation attempts to convey this by 'we', because the effect of the French is to blur the distinctions of persons).

'Pleindre' once more has multiple echoes: in *12*.12–13 we even had 'pleinte' rhyming with 'contreinte'. 'Contreindre' shows that she wishes to abrogate responsibility, but she has told us enough already to make it clear that she has no need at all of constraint.

Line 5 is something more than a statement of Louise's own personal inability to take part in social and courtly life in the absence of the lover; it also fits in to the general trend of satire, common at the time, on the artificiality of court-life, an excellent example of which is the treatment Du Bellay gives it in some of his *Regrets*. Louise Labé adds to this the contrast she makes between the artificiality and pretence, and her own experience of love, thus stressing once again that she is not writing poetry simply because it was a fashionable pursuit.

The sounds '*tour*nois' and 'jeus' are common ones in her poetry ('*tour*nois' links with all the references to 'tours' and 'jours' we have already seen, and 'jeus' goes back through 'mieus' and 'lieus' of this poem to 'feu peu hatif' of *16*.10 and to 'mile jeus' of *15*.9; 'jeus' is also very much a key sound in the present sonnet, because apart from the rhymes we find 'Tu peus' and 'je veus'). In l.6 'sans toy' contrasts with the equally strong use of 'avec toy' in *14*.2 and the other instances of 'avec' with a pronoun, e.g., 'avec moy' (*12*.4), 'avec lui' (*13*.3). It is worth noting the importance for her of this simple expression of human relationship, either of union or separation.

'Peindre' (often used at the time to mean 'imagine') shows the creativity of love, the inspiration which the lover is able to provide; usually in poetry the woman is the one who inspires, but only because the writers were usually men, cf. *Élégie* 11, ll.81–2: 'Tu es tout seul, tout mon mal et mon bien:/Avec toy tout, et sans toy je n'ay rien': [You alone are my suffering and my happiness; with you I have everything, without you nothing.]

'Un nouvel obget' refers back to 'divertissements' in l.5. She does try to find some escape ('tachant à ce desir esteindre') though she is not looking for someone else, but for a relief from love itself ('Et des pensers amoureus me distraire').

We may compare Ronsard, *Amours.* s.*23*, ll.1–11:

Ce beau corail, ce marbre qui souspire . . .

Me sont au cœur en si profond esmoy'

Qu'un autre object ne se présente à moy,

Sinon le beau de leur beau que j'adore.

[This beautiful coral, this breathing marble . . . bring such emotion to my heart that no other object presents itself to me except the beauty of their beauty which I adore.]

Weber, in his edition of the *Amours*, compares this with Petrarch's CCXXVI, ll.3–4 '. . . nè quest' occhi hann' altro obietto'. Cotgrave gives for *Object*: 'An obiect, the subiect of the sight; any thing one lookes on directly; anything that is before the eyes'; cf. Magny, *Les amours*, s.*57*:

De tant de traits Amour trop irrité

De decocher sur moy se trauailla:

Lors que de vous l'obget il me bailla,

Pour vous seruir en toute integrité.

[Love, annoyed by all the arrows he had to carry, set about firing at me; he presented me with you, to serve you faithfully.]

(Once we have the *sounds* of these poems in our head we are able to cross-refer between the poems; rhyme is much more than what we find at the end of the lines; here, for example, 'Et des pensers' can be said to *rhyme* with the similarly placed 'Sans y penser' of *8*.11).

Line 10 is purely Petrarch in idea; cf. Ronsard, *Amours*, s.*155*, ll.12–14;

Seul, et pensif, aux rochers plus segretz,

D'un cuœur muet je conte mes regretz,
Et par les boys je voys celant ma playe.
[Alone, and thoughtful, I tell my sorrows in silence to the
most hidden rocks, and go through the woods concealing
my wound.]

'Sui' presents some difficulty, whether we take it as part of
'être' or of 'suivre'; if it is 'être' then it is odd to find '*le* plus
. . .', and 'suivre' does not seem to be used in this way.

In l.11 we see in 'Mais' a strong adversative link between the
parts of the sonnet; this is a common device in Louise Labé
(cf. *11*.11, *12*.11, *14*.10, etc.).

'Hors de moymesme vivre' is not at first clear since living
outside herself seems to mean for her living in ecstasy. Here she
is living outside herself in a different way to sonnets *9* and *13*.
Now she is saying that he is so much part of her that the only
way in which she can escape from him is by escaping from herself. 'Sejour' recalls 'ce mortel sejour' of *14*.12. This last line is
odd since the main reason for her unhappiness is that he has
already gone away. She is well aware that absence does not
free her from him. (Or is it that this poem refers to a different
situation, and that the lover is living nearby?).*

This last line has elicited some very different interpretations.
'Ou' has been read as 'où' ('where' instead of 'or'); this does
not seem plausible. Then 'fais' and 'sois' are ambiguous, because of the omission of the pronouns. 'Fais' could be an imperative, or its subject could be either Louise or her lover.

SONNET 18

This is the most celebrated and most often anthologized of the
sonnets, and at the same time, and for the same reason, is the
least easy to comment on. It both belongs to, and stands aside
from, the tradition of poetry on the theme of kissing (cf., for
example, Catullus' *Da mihi basia*).

The intimate colloquial style relies on the simple ono-
matopœic expressions (above all the sounds 'm', 'b', 's', 'v').
The immediacy of the first line is partly due to the reference to
previous kissing ('encor'), and because it brooks no refusal;
the second line suggests the familiarity of many different
kinds of kiss. 'Rebaise' is not of course a new coinage in the
language of Louise Labé (it is used, for example, by Lemaire de

Belges, and by Ronsard in the *Amours de Marie*, and it was a common prefix in the middle ages).

The whole poem is a mixture of exhortation, command, wish, and promise and owes much to the use of memory in recreating the experience. There is a very careful structure (cf. the parallelism of ll.2–3, and the way in which the first quatrain is formed round the sound '*m'en*cor', '*m'en* un', '*t'en* un' which also reappears in l.6). The use of superlatives (ll.2–3) makes for greater intensity. 'Savoureux', a common adjective with 'baiser' (cf. Ronsard, *Amours*, s.*55*) recalls *13*.12, 'Lors que souef plus il me baiseroit' and through this line the whole of s.*13* with its sensual harmony and fulfilment. The playful l.5 recalls *12*.14, 'Et d'un dous mal douce fin esperer', 'ennui moderer' (*15*.8) and 'consolé' (*16*.9).

The end of the second quatrain sums up the sensuality of ll. 1–6, and carries it further by its generality. Line 8 follows closely *13*.6 'Contentons nous l'un l'autre', and 'aise' also appears in s.*13* and 'contentement' in the present one, making the two sonnets even closer.

The tercets make explicit the life the lovers can enjoy in each other. This was a commonplace—cf. Ronsard, *Amours*, s.*135*, ll.9–11: 'En toy je suis, et tu es dedans moy,/En moy tu vis, et je vis dedans toy:/Ainsi noz toutz ne font qu'un petit monde.' [I am within you and you within me, In me you live and I in you: thus our whole selves make up but one little world.]

In l.10 there is a partial ambiguity since we are tempted to read 'son amy vivra' as an absolute phrase and not as standing for 'et en son amy vivra', thus putting the accent on continuing life in contrast to the death-wish of some of the earlier sonnets. 'Permets m'Amour' needs some attention: it could stand for 'Permets-moy, Amour' or for 'Permets, mon Amour', cf., below, *22*.2 't'Amie'; in either case, love or Love must be a vocative.

'Quelque folie' is the folly or madness of being in love, (Venus, in *Le débat de folie et d'amour*, calls Folie 'la plus outrageuse Furie qui onques fut ez Enfers' [the fiercest Fury who ever was in Hell]) and the particular acts of folly to which it gives rise; it is also the lack of reason involved in writing erotic fantasies such as this one. Cotgrave gives for *Folie*: 'Follie, simplicitie, foolishnesse, fondnesse, unadvisednesse, foppishnesse, indiscretion, ideotisme'. He gives also '*Folie aux garçons*: Lecherie; and hence; *Faire folie* A woman to play false, enter a man more than she ought, or tread her shooe awry'. Finally he notes the proverb '*Folie faire, et folie recognoistre, sont deux pairs de folie*; Hee's doubly fond that justifies his fondnesse'. In this poem Louise Labé shows herself doubly fond. '*Vivant discretement*' (Estienne, 'Prudenter'; Cotgrave 'Discreetly, advisedly; prudently; providently, heedfully, circumspectly'; Huguet 'avec discernement, sagement') has a triple reference, (i) living without kissing (ii) living without loving at all (iii) writing poetry which is not passionate: this sonnet represents the opposite of this. The last line refers again to her going outside herself (there is a very clear reference to s.*17*), but this time the two meanings are joined, i.e., escape and ecstasy. '*Saillie*' according to Huguet has three meanings: 'action de sortir, sortie: sortie pour attaquer l'ennemi: digression'. All these meanings are present here (for the second, cf. *4.9*, 'assaillir') Cotgrave has: 'A sallie, eruption, violent issue, or breaking out upon, also, a leap, [etc.,] . . . any disordinate excesse, or excessive out-standing.'

Some of the phrases which Cotgrave gives for *saillie* help to explain Louise's meaning here: '*Il a fait une saillie*. He hath runne too much riot; he hath made a foule fault; he was ill overseene, or too far carried by haste, choller, passion, foolish or haire-braind affection', and, '*Il a les plus plaisantes saillies du monde*: He uses the most prettie, odde, and extravagant digressions that ever I heard'. It should perhaps be noted also that *saillir* is translated by Cotgrave, in one of its meanings, as 'to ride, or leap one another, as the male doth the female'. Harvey, in commenting on the last quatrain of this sonnet, says

> These lines add a note of suffering that comes with separation from the beloved (*discrettement* in the sense of 'apart'). They seek to evoke pity and to check the beloved's complaints. The *saillie*, for this sense, refers back to the Platonic 'chacun en soy et son ami vivra'. At the same time the narrator tries not to be too serious and counters her philosophizing and her anxiety with a playful, whimsical note. She makes fun of her own rhetoric, her *folie* and explains that the Platonic image of a literal

going outside the self is only verbal play (*a saillie*) that relieves the reserved, discreet mode of her existence.[16]

I wonder if we might also compare Montaigne's comment in I. XXIV:

> Or je dy que, non en la medecine seulement, mais en plusieurs arts plus certaines, la fortune y a bonne part. Les saillies poëtiques, qui emportent leur autheur et le ravissent hors de soy, pourquoy ne les attribuerons nous à son bonheur? puis qu'il confesse luy mesme qu'elles surpassent sa suffisance et ses forces, et les reconnoit venir d'ailleurs que de soy, et ne les avoir aucunement en sa puissance; non plus que les orateurs ne disent avoir en la leur ces mouvemens et agitations extraordinaires, qui les poussent au delà de leur dessein.
>
> [So I say that, not only in medicine, but in many more reliable arts, chance plays a large part. Why should we not attribute poetic sallies, which carry their author away and take him out of himself, to his good fortune? He says himself that they go beyond his competence and his strength, and he recognizes that they come from outside himself, and are not within his control; in the same way as orators do not claim to have power over those extraordinary movements and agitations which push them further than they intended.]

SONNET 19

After the impassioned involvement of s.*18* this sonnet appears utterly detached; this is partly the result of the mythological setting, which ensures that the tone is the same as that of the *Débat de folie et d'amour*.

'L'espesseur d'un bois' takes up the idea of *17*.10, 'Des bois espais sui le plus solitaire'.

The mythology in the present sonnet is better integrated with the rest of the poem than it was in s.*16*, for although there is a direct distinction made between the narrator of the poem and the goddess (J'allois resvant'), the fiction of the dialogue is maintained to the end of the piece. Line 4 unites the mythological and the more real elements, giving each of these some of the qualities of the other. The continuous nature of the tense recalls 'vois mourant' (*13*.2); 'comme fay maintefois' and 'Sans y penser' ('machinalement') bring out the common-place element in what is being described.

The 'vois' is presumably that of Diana herself, unless it belongs to one of the nymphs. 'Nynfe estonnee' is economical, telling us in direct speech of her surprise and Diana's aware-ness of it; the voice immediately associates Louise (or her *persona* in the poem) with the mythological nymphs. I do not think that Louise Labé wishes to make much of the mytho-logy here, in spite of all the implications of the myth of Diana, since she treats it so lightly. Scève did make much of this myth in the *Délie*, but his interest in the underlying symbolism was deeper. In ll.6–8 the point is that Diana is the one goddess not affected by love, the goddess of chastity. Calepin (fol-lowed closely by Charles Estienne) says of Diana in his dictionary:

> Haec ob virginitatis amorem fertur hominum consortia fugisse: et ut à se libidinis pruritum amoueret, venando syluas incoluisse, paucarum virginum comitatu contenta. Arcum ferebat et pharetram, succincta semper incedens, et cothurno induta. Ob hanc causam syluarum et nemorum dea putabatur. . . . [She is said to have fled the company of men because of her love of virginity, and in order to escape the promptings of lust, to have dwelt in the woods as a huntress, content with the company of a few virgins. She used to carry a bow and a quiver, always walking with her skirts tucked up, and wearing hunting boots. Because of this she was thought to be goddess of the woods and groves . . .]

'Qu'as-tu trouvé, ô compagne, en ta voye?' is very like the medieval liturgical sequence for Easter Day: 'Dic nobis, Maria, quid vidisti in via?'. [Tell us, Mary, what you saw on your way?] I am not certain whether it became a technique of dialogue pieces or whether it was just a personal recollec-tion of the author.

The last four lines turn the direction of the poem round, and return us to the 'real life' of her experience. The direct-ness and personal nature of these lines come out also in the change of tense contained in 'Je m'animay'. We, the readers, know that 'à un passant' is somewhat less than truthful (the word has been used once already in *15*.8 in a general sense); her lover was much more than this, but she is being

deliberately detached and off-hand. 'En vain', too, is an under-
statement, because of all the echoes of 'nuits vainement
atendues'—and remember that Diana was the moon-goddess.
Apart from the humour of situation in 'l'arc apres', we see that
there are no limits to this total love which she tried to make
him return.

The final 'mais' comes later in the poem than usual, thus
intensifying the 'pointe'. There is a wistful yet violent falling
rhythm in 'cent et cent bresches'; for the idea of the wounds
of love cf. 'Tal piaga' (*1*.6) and 'une nouvelle plaie' (*3*.13);
as in *Élégie* III, (ll.65–6)

> La bresche faite, entre Amour en la place,
> Dont le repos premierement il chasse:
> [When the wound is made, Love enters in, and the first
> thing he does is to banish rest.]

This sonnet may be compared with Scève, *Délie, 327*,

'Délie aux champs troussée, et accoustrée', in which
Délie meets love, and says she does not need any other weapons
than her own eyes.

SONNET 20

The first line of this sonnet has occasioned some difficulty.
The first edition reads 'devoit' and so does the 1556 edition
which claims that it contains the author's corrections to the
first edition. Many modern editors, however, correct the text
so that it reads 'devois'. Luc van Brabant shows that Boy in
1887 was responsible for the emendation, but talks as though
it was simply a misreading of the text, instead of an attempt
to correct an error and give better sense. The reading 'devoit'
seems to be confirmed by l.5, 'le voyant aymer fatalement';
there is no reason why she should love him in return but she
does so out of pity. On the other hand, if we read 'devois'
this gives better sense to 'sans autre peinture/Le reconnu
quand vy premierement': 'reconnu' then would indicate that
her recognition and love were simultaneous.

This is a narrative poem about the inevitability of predestined
love, which intensifies the torment of it. The exact time of
'fut' is not clear, but in l.2 'un jour' suggests that it was not in
the recent past. Nor is it clear how the prediction was supposed to have taken place. Was it perhaps in a dream?

Prophecy, it will be remembered, was one of the four kinds of 'fureur': ('La troisieme par ravissement de prophetie, vaticination, ou divination souz Apollon').[17] 'Le reconnu' suggests something more than just love at first sight: it involves a Platonic recognition of what has already been glimpsed in another existence. This ties in with one contemporary theory that all love involved such recognition (cf., for example, Héroët, *La parfaicte amye*). 'Premierement' does indeed take us back to the beginning (cf. *4*.1–2, 'Depuis qu'Amour cruel empoisonna/Premierement . . .').

The second quatrain begins with a description of situation which is similar to the one in *19*.13–14 ('mais lui, les ramassant'). Line 7, 'Et tellement je forçay ma nature', coming after the earnest longing of sonnets 1–19, is surely ironical, unless she wishes to say that she was not like this before the coming of love. Somehow we do not imagine that such love goes against her own passionately sensual nature. (Perhaps it was supposed to be woman's nature not to love. But she sees herself as distinct from this nature).*

Perhaps proof of the suggestion that she is talking of the change brought about by love is to be found in *Le débat*:

> Il faut confesser qu'incontinent que cette passion vient saisir l'homme, elle l'altère et immue. Car le desir incessamment se demeine dedens l'ame, la poignant tousjours et resveillant. Cette agitacion d'esprit, si elle estoit naturelle, elle ne l'afligeroit de la sorte qu'elle fait: mais estant contre son naturel, elle le malmeine, en sorte qu'il se fait tout autre qu'il n'estoit. [It must be said that as soon as this passion comes and takes hold of a man, it changes and transforms him. For desire moves continually in his mind, pricking it and wakening it. If this agitation of the spirit were natural, it would not afflict him as much as it does. But since it goes against his nature, it maltreats him, so that he becomes quite different from what he was.]

In the tercets she states that such divinely ordained and inspired love should be pleasant, but that she feels the influence of some cruel demonic power. In her use of the storm imagery in ll.11–12 we may notice that 'horrible' has a strong Latin sense (synonymous with 'horrendus'); Huguet gives 'terrible, effrayant, redoutable, effrayant pour l'imagination'; the word had begun to take on its modern diluted meaning,

perhaps through the influence of Rabelais who used it often
in a neutral sense with humorous intention, e.g., 'Puis beut
un horrible traict de vin. . . .'[18] [Then he drank a horrible
draught of wine. . . .]. 'M'ourdissoient ce naufrage' is not
so much a mixed metaphor as an expression which contains a
metaphor ('naufrage') and a dead metaphor, since 'ourdir'
was already being used in the sense of 'fabriquer, faire':
Cotgrave gives for *ourdir*: 'To warpe a web of cloth, to lay
the warpe thereof, or put it into the loome; to beginne a web,
to beginne to weave; (hence) also, to invent, contrive, begin,
cause, procure'.

SONNET 21

This simple reflective poem loses a little because of its gratuit-
ous expansiveness.

In her list of questions about the nature of physical and spiritual attraction the author uses many words which refer obviously to the descriptions we have already met in the sonnets.

Luc van Brabant has some interesting things to say about
this sonnet. He is of the opinion that the questions are not all
parallel. For him ll.3–4 are *answers* to the questions in ll.1–2,
and ll.6–7 are *answers* to l.5. This depends on a reading of
'Qui' as standing for 'Celui qui'; the lines which are to be
taken as answers would then begin, 'Is it the one which . . .'
This use of 'Qui' is, as he pointed out, found in Olivier de
Magny, and in Louise Labé herself, (s.*6*, 'Qu'elle pourroit se
vanter . . . (celle) qui baiseroit'). In the contrast contained
in these lines Van Brabant sees a comparison between the two
supposed lovers, Magny and Henri II, in which the references
to pain and unrequited love concern Henri. 'Emmieleur'
means seductive, and here, according to the same critic,
refers to Magny.

In l.8 the question 'Quel naturel est le plus amiable?' is
generic and sums up all the preceding questions; we are
reminded of *20*.7 'Et tellement je forçay ma nature' (cf., also,
later in this present poem 'Ayant Amour forcé mon jugement').
'Jugement' in the sixteenth century, and especially in Montaigne who has much to say about it, was considered to be
essentially a natural, innate quality (Estienne has, 'Ce iuge-
ment et raison dont tous les hommes ont participation, Sensus

communis'). [That power of judgement and reason which all men share, Common Sense.]

In the emphatic l.11 the confident assertion ('Mais je say bien') gains force by the variation from 'assurément' to 'je m'assure'. In l.12 'tout le beau' is absolute and all-inclusive, and is to be compared with *17*.6, 'Rien sans toy de beau ne me puis peindre'. The relationship between art and nature, and especially in the matter of poetic theory, was one which was debated very earnestly during the years immediately preceding the appearance of these sonnets. One of the most important statements of the problem was the one written by Jacques Peletier du Mans in his *Art poëtique*, published in Lyon in the same year as Louise's book, and by the same publisher. 'Art' very often means, in this context, 'artifice' or 'crafts-manship'. The last line expresses the absoluteness and climax of her desire, which is equal to the climax of her misery and torment: this often appears in the last lines of the sonnets, for example, sonnets *3*, *5* and *13*. 'Acroitre' recalls *3*.8 ('Estimez vous croitre encore mes peines ?') and *20*.9 ('en faveur devoit croitre'). In all these instances she shows an awareness of the possibility of growth, development, movement in her exper-ience, though at the same time she denies it.

SONNET 22
This is the most mythological of the sonnets but there is nothing academic or obscure in this use of classical allusion. The meaning of the mythological elements is clear and uni-form, and the subsequent application to her own situation is equally so. There is variety in the description of the love which the divine beings have for their lovers, which is mirrored in the varied sentence structure and length. (The short 'Mars voit Venus', for example, makes even swifter the following movements of Mercury).

It should be noted that Endymion, the beautiful shepherd, put by Jupiter into an eternal sleep, was loved by the moon (cf. Scève, *Délie*, *126*).

In the first quatrain we must understand 'Et toy . . . (tu es bien heureus)/Tant te repais . . .' 'Se glasse' is a rare form of 'se glisse'. With the mention of Mercury the stress is changed from the happy fruition of love to the ability to find love (Mercury) or to remember it (Jupiter). The point of contact with the first quatrain is that all these figures find harmony, even the adulterous Mars. There is music in the spheres and it is caused by love (though it is not Dante's 'love which moves the sun and the other stars').

The application to herself is held over to the last line. It has been suggested that 'travailler' here has the meaning of 'souffrir' which it often had at the time and in the work of Louise Labé, but it should also be taken literally since 'travailler en vain' was often used as a set phrase (cf. many illustrations in Estienne's dictionary).

The idea of cosmic harmony based on love is to be found also in *Le débat*:

> Si tout l'Univers ne tient que par certaines amoureuses composicions, si elles cessoient, l'ancien Abime reviendroit. Otant l'amour, tout est ruiné. [If the whole Universe is held together only by a certain amorous harmony, if this ceased, the ancient Chaos would return. Take away love, and all is ruined.]

SONNET 23

After starting off in a mood of tired melancholy this poem turns first to bitterness (l.9), and then to a mood of repentance in which the author asks the lover's pardon, since she realizes (l.11) his suffering may be equal to her own. 'Jadis' seems to refer to a fairly distant past. The praise described in ll.2–5 is often taken to be a direct reference to a poem of Olivier de Magny

> Où print l'enfant Amour le fin or qui dora
> En mille crespillons ta teste blondissante ?
> [Where did the child Love get the fine gold which coloured your head with a thousand golden curls ?]

contained in the *Escriz de divers poëtes, à la louenge de Louize Labé Lionnoize*, published with the Sonnets, and also s.*32* of the *Soupirs* (1557), but it is surely general enough to apply to a great number of love-poems. The speed of ll.1–5, with the double enjambement of 3/4/5, shows that she is conscious that she is quoting (especially in ll.4–5) either an actual poem or a fictitious traditional Petrarchan poem. She is also, too, in a sense, quoting herself: cf., for example, *3*.9–10, 'Qu'encor

Amour sur moy son arc essaie,/Que nouveaus feus me gette et nouveaus dars', and the whole of sonnet *19*.

In ll.6–8 she attacks the lover's infidelity, or at least his indifference and insincerity. She is also attacking here the excesses of Petrarchan love-poetry, rather in the same way as Du Bellay had done in *À une dame* (1553). Her own tears, too, are short-lived, but for a different reason—because she is subject to extremes of joy and pain. 'Ferme amour' recalls precisely 'devoit fermement/Un jour aymer' (*20*.1–2). 'Finement' contains the idea of malicious cunning (cf., among the many equivalents given in Estienne, 'Astutè, Callidè, Cautè, Malitiosè').

In l.9 'Le but de ta malice' is addressed both to Love and to the lover. 'De m'asservir sous ombre de service' is perhaps a stock idea, but after reading these poems we have gained the very distinct impression that it is an apt one. In spite of his indifference she is unable to escape from him, cf. the end of s.*17*. The change of mood in ll.11–14 shows the same fine analysis of feelings as did the end of s.*7*. She explains her bitterness on the grounds that she is in a state of despair, 'Estant outree et de despit et d'ire'. Cotgrave gives for *outré*: 'Pierced, bored, struck thorow, run thorow and thorow'. For *oultré* he gives the same meanings, and adds 'also, sicklie, unsound, or consumed in bodie' and then *oultré d'amour* 'Farre gone, over head and eares, in love'. I do not know that we can make much distinction between *despit* and *ire*. Cotgrave has, for the former, 'Despight, spight, anger, spleen, stomacke, vexation', and for the latter, 'Ire, anger, choler, chafing, fuming, pettishnesse, wrath, rage, moodinesse, indignation.' As in s.*7* she is ready to find excuses for him and for his absence. 'Mais je m'assure' might suggest that she is protesting too much, but I feel that it is rather a conversational repetition of words and ideas just discovered (cf. *21*.11) and found comforting.

At the end of this sonnet the lover has become a *little* less shadowy and illusory, but we are still not much nearer knowing why he does not reappear, why he has rejected her, or even if he has rejected her. He lives only through her eyes, only through the picture she gives us of him. This, it seems to me, makes it profoundly irrelevant to work out how much refers to Henri II and how much to Olivier de Magny.

What matters is the love-experience created, not just re-created, by the poem.

'Qu'autant que moy' reminds us of 'Qu'autant que lui' (*20*.8): her fondness for comparison is a way of associating herself with her lover, and of seeing them both with reference to an ideal and absolute love.

SONNET 24

Although very little of this sequence is based on anecdote, and so lacks a chronological order of presentation, there is nonetheless a clear beginning and end. Sonnet *24* concludes the work by setting it against the social background, of her own time, but also of all time. The tense ('si j'ay aymé') is important, referring to the actual experience and to its des-cription in the poem; the other tenses are important, too; present and future are contrasted with the past tense of ex-perience. The word 'si' is used in different senses in the poem: in ll.1, 2 and 4 it has no hypothetical force at all for someone who has read through these sonnets, but means 'that' or 'because'.

In l.6 there is ambiguity; we expect at first that it has the same meaning as the parallel in l.1, but again someone who has read the poems is unable to imagine that Louise Labé thinks that she has failed in any way. It is possible also that it means 'committed a fault (against conventional rules)'. In l.11 'si' is used in the ordinary conditional sense.

Lines 2–3 sum up the sequence by means of trite expres-sions, just as sonnets *1* and *2* had summed it up in advance, especially 'O mile morts en mile rets tendues' (*2*.7) and 'Tant de flambeaux pour ardre une femmelle!' (*2*.11). 'Travaus', in the sense of 'suffering' recalls many poems (*4*.5, *5*.4, *5*.8, for example). Line 4 ('en pleurant') describes both her love-affair and her love-poetry.

This final poem is deeply concerned with time and its relation to her experience: ('mon tems'; cf. 'mes cours jours' (*13*.4)). 'Consumé' suggests also that she has been consumed by time in the same way as she has been burned ('ardentes') or eaten up ('mordentes') by her sorrow.

'Mon nom' (l.5) is her reputation, both in her present life and in the life which her poetry has given, and will continue to give her. Cotgrave has 'Nom: A name; the tearm or title, whereby a thing is called, also, a fame, bruit, report; whence; *Il en a le nom'*.

In l.6 ('Si j'ay failli') there is a hint of doubt whether she thinks her love to have been a transgression (except in conventional terms). There is a very close similarity with the third *Élégie*, also addressed to the Dames Lionnoises, (ll.5–7):

Ne veuillez point condamner ma simplesse,

Et jeune erreur de ma fole jeunesse,

Si c'est erreur:

[Please do not condemn my simplicity, and the youthful error of my foolish youth—if error it is.]

In the second *Élégie* she says, talking of God, that her only vice has been to have adored her lover as God.

In the third *Élégie* she tries to show that she is no more 'vicious' than anyone else; she lists the discontented, the envious, the war-like, the avaricious, perjurors, liars, the covetous, and concludes (ll.27–8):

Mais si en moy rien y ha d'imparfait,

Qu'on blame Amour: c'est lui seul qui l'a fait.

[But if there is anything imperfect in me, Love is to blame; he alone is responsible.]

She even allies herself, in a way, with the other women, in making Love say to her (ll.46–7):

Tu penses donq, ô Lyonnoise Dame,

Pouvoir fuir par ce moyen ma flame:

[You think therefore, woman of Lyons, that you can escape my flame in this way.]

To return to s.*24*—with the author we have experienced 'les peines presentes' in the poems, and have seen something of the violence and tempestuousness of this poetry. There is a strong, but controlled, flowing movement throughout this last sonnet, with its mixture of enjambement (note how far 'pourra' is from 'Amour') and self-contained lines.

I do not agree with Giudici's comment that, because of the unnecessary alliteration, the bad taste of l.7 is undeniable.[19] In this poem she *is* detached from her experience and so is able to stand apart even from the language she uses. She is in perfect control of the situation.

The meaning of ll.9–11 is not absolutely clear, but it seems to be: 'without having the excuse for your ardour that your lover is like Vulcan, and without appealing to his beauty

which is like that of Adonis'. In other words, you could fall a
prey to passion without having anything like the excuse that
I have. There is also the powerful suggestion that her own
lover is both Vulcan and Adonis.

The reference to Adonis is perhaps simple enough. The
contemporary mythological dictionaries talk about his legend-
ary beauty. Vulcan, however, causes some difficulty. Certainly there is a reference to the fires of the divine blacksmith.
There is also a tradition according to which Vulcan is depicted
as the old and jealous husband (and the parallel with Louise's
case is obvious). This tradition was known at the time; cf.
Scève, *Délie, 83*: 'Vulcan ialoux reprochoit a sa femme,/Que
son enfant causoit son vitupere', and Ronsard, *Amours*, s.*190*,
ll.11–14:

> Hà, que je porte et de haine et d'envie
> A ce Vulcan ingrat et sans pitié,
> Qui s'opposant aux rais de ma moitié,
> Fait éclipser le soleil de ma vie.

> [Ah, what hatred and jealousy I bear for this thankless
> and heartless Vulcan who opposes the rays of my better
> half, and eclipses the sun of my life.]

All the mythological dictionaries (Torrentin, Calepin,
Charles Estienne) relate Vulcan's marriage to Venus, her
infidelity with Mars, and Vulcan's punishment of them. If
this interpretation is followed here, then the meaning would
be 'without being able to excuse your ardour because of the
existence of a jealous husband'. I give this explanation as a
possible one though I do not believe it to be correct. It seems
to me that this imagery might be too complicated for Louise
Labé, and that for her Vulcan simply suggests the fiery or
'ardent' element in love.

Line 11 is emphatic because 'pourra' is future and not conditional. They could, with less justification, be more subject to
passion than she has been; cf. *Élégie* 1, ll.37–8: 'Je n'aperçu
que soudein me vint prendre/Le mesme mal que je soulois
reprendre'. [I had no sooner seen him than I was overcome
by the same sickness I used to reproach in others.]

Her account of how she first despised Love and was then
conquered should serve as a convincing example to the ladies
of Lyon. Notice especially 'mal' and 'reprendre' which reappear in s.*24*.

Élégie I is also an interesting commentary on the present sonnet. It even addresses the 'Lionnoises' (ll.43–4):

> Dames, qui les lirez,
>
> De mes regrets avec moy soupirez.

In the *Élégie* she goes further than in the sonnet, saying that she may even lament with them:

> Possible, un jour je feray le semblable,
>
> Et ayderay votre voix pitoyable
>
> A vos travaus et peines raconter,
>
> Au tems perdu vainement lamenter. (ll.45–8)

This ties in with Harvey's idea that *24*.14 contains an element of pity.[20] In the *Élégie* she amplifies ll.11–14 of the sonnet:

> Quelque rigueur qui loge en votre cœur,
>
> Amour s'en peut un jour rendre vainqueur.
>
> Et plus aurez lui esté ennemies,
>
> Pis vous fera, vous sentant asservies. (ll.49–52)

In the second last line of s.*24*,

> Et plus d'estrange et forte passion,

the word 'estrange' refers indirectly to ss.*17* and *18* 'hors de moy'. So in *Élégie* I, (ll.88–9), we read,

> Ainsi Amour de toy t'a estrangee
>
> Qu'on te diroit en une autre changee.

> ['Ladies who will read my poems, you will lament my grief with me'; 'Perhaps one day I'll do the same for you, and help your pitiful voice when it relates your troubles and suffering, and vainly laments the wasted past'. 'Whatever hardness dwells in your heart, Love may some day conquer it; and the more hostile you have been to him, the worse he will treat you who are now his slaves'. 'So Love has estranged you from yourself, so that one would say you've been changed into another person'.]

The main difference between this first *Élégie* and s.*24* is that the *Élégie* adds the example of the love of Queen Semiramis, and adds a *carpe diem* argument that it is no use loving when it is too late, because the object of one's love will be horrified by the excessive make-up which will be necessary. (The last line sums up the whole sequence. It comes almost as an afterthought, driving home the point she has already made in line 13, at the same time as she appeals once again for their pity, she warns them with an even more convincing argument).*

NOTES

1 Nicholas, B. L., 'The Uses of the Sonnet: Louise Labé and Du Bellay', in *French Literature and its background* (I), 100.

2 Giudici, II, 230.

3 1956, 508–10.

4 Ronsard, *Œuvres complètes*, ed. G. Cohen (Paris, 1950) 288.

5 Van Brabant, *De Vijfentwintig Sonnetten*, 77, 80–1.

6 Cf. Robinson, D.M., *Sappho and her influence* (London, n.d.) 161.

7 O'Connor, *Louise Labé, sa vie et son œuvre*, 137; Van Brabant, op. cit., 81.

8 Giudici, I, 263.

9 Merrill, R.V., and Clements, R.J., *Platonism in French Renaissance Poetry*, (New York, 1957) 117.

10 Saulnier, *Maurice Scève* I, 237–8.

11 Cf. Joukovsky, Françoise, *Orphée et ses disciples dans la poésie française et néo-latine du XVIe siècle* (Geneva, 1970).

12 Giudici, II, 449.

13 Du Bellay, *Œuvres poétiques*, IV, 130.

14 Ed. *Amours*, 592.

15 Giudici, II, 259; 240.

16 Harvey, *The Aesthetics of the Renaissance Love-Sonnet*, 76.

17 Pontus de Tyard, *Le Solitaire Premier*, ed. Silvio Baridon (Geneva, 1950) 17.

18 Rabelais, *Gargantua*, ch. 38.

19 Giudici, I, 106.

20 Harvey, 'A Poetic *Envoi* considered as Art' in *Modern Language Notes* (1959) 118–23.

SELECT BIBLIOGRAPHY

1 *Editions and translations of Louise Labé*

    Euvres. Lyon, 1555 (BN. Rés. Ye 1651); The present edition is based on this first edition. There were three other editions in her lifetime, in 1556, especially *Euvres de Louïze Labé Lyonnoïze revues et corrigées par ladite Dame*, Lyon, 1556 (BM. G.18078). There are a few minor variants.

    Œuvres, ed. Charles Boy. Paris, 1877; (Slatkine reprints, 1968).

    Œuvres, ed. Seheur. Paris, 1927.

    Love Sonnets, trans. by Frederic Prokosch. New York, 1947.

    Sonnets, trans. by Alta Lind Cook. Toronto, 1950.

    The Twenty-Four Love Sonnets, trans. by Frances Lobb. London 1950.

    Sonnets, trans. by J. Edgardo Rivera Martinez. Lima, 1960.

    De Vijfentwintig Sonnetten van Louïze Labé, trans. with a commentary, by Luc van Brabant. Amsterdam, 1960.

    The Sonnets, trans. by Bettina L. Knapp. Paris, 1964.

    Poems from Œuvres: 1556, French Renaissance Students' Facsimiles, ed. Kenneth Varty, Scolar Press, Menston, 1971.

2 *Books and articles on Louise Labé and related topics*

    Giudici, Enzo, *Il Canzoniere, La Disputa di Follia e di Amore*. Parma, 1955; (referred to in the notes as 'Giudici I').

    — *Louise Labé e l'École lyonnaise*. Naples, 1964; (referred to in the notes as 'Giudici II').

    — *Amore e follia nell' opera della 'Belle Cordière'*. Naples, 1965.

    — *Spiritualismo e Carnascialismo*, I, Naples, 1968.

    Guillot, G., *Un tableau synoptique de la vie et des œuvres de Louise Labé*. Paris, 1962.

    Harvey, Laurence, *The Aesthetics of the Renaissance Love-Sonnet; an essay in the art of the sonnet in the poetry of Louise Labé*. Geneva, 1962.

    MacFarlane, Ian D. Edition of Scève's *Délie*. Cambridge 1966.

    Nicholas, Brian, 'The Uses of the Sonnet: Louise Labé and Du Bellay', in *French Literature and its background* (1): *The Sixteenth Century*, ed. John Cruickshank. London, 1968.

    O'Connor, Dorothy, *Louise Labé, sa vie et son œuvre*. Paris, 1926.

    Petrey, Sandy, 'The Character of the Speaker in the Poetry of Louise Labé', in *The French Review*, XLIII (March, 1970) 588–96.

    Ronsard, Pierre de, *Les Amours*, ed. H. et C. Weber. Paris, 1963.

    Saulnier, Verdun, *Maurice Scève*, 2 vols. Paris, 1948.

Varty, Kenneth, 'Louise Labé's theory of transformation', in
French Studies, XII (January, 1958) 5-13.

— 'The life and legend of Louise Labé', in *Nottingham
Medieval Studies*, III (1959) 78-108.

Zamaron, Fernand, *Louise Labé, Dame de Franchise*. Paris,
1968.

3 *Dictionaries*

Calepin, A., *Dictionarium, quarto et postremo ex R. Stephani
Latinae Linguae Thesauro auctum*. Paris, 1553-4.

Cotgrave, R., *A Dictionarie of the French and English Tongues*.
London, 1611.

Estienne, C., *A Dictionarium historicum ac poeticum*. Paris,
1553.

Estienne, R., *Dictionnaire françois latin*. Paris, 1549.

Huguet, E., *Dictionnaire de la langue française du seizième siècle*.
Paris, 1925-67.

Palsgrave, J., *Lesclarcissement de la langue françoyse*. London,
1530.

Torrentin, H., *Dictionarium poeticum quod vulgo inscribitur
Elucidarius Carminum*. Paris (R. Estienne) 1530; Bâle, 1552.

FIRST LINES